TRIALS AND TRIBULATIONS

Wisdom & Benefits

by

al-Imām al-ʿIzz bin ʿAbdi-s-Salām (d. 660H)

with an appendix from the work of

al-Ḥāfiẓ ibn al-Qayyim (d. 751H)

Translated from the original Arabic by

Abū Rumaysah

DAAR US-SUNNAH PUBLISHERS

Title:
TRIALS AND TRIBULATIONS
Wisdom and Benefits

by
al-Imām al-'Izz bin 'Abdi-s-Salām (d. 660H)

with an appendix from the work of
al-Ḥāfiẓ ibn al-Qayyim (d. 751H)

Translated from the original Arabic by Abū Rumaysah

All inquiries must be addressed to:

Daar us-Sunnah Publishers
P.O. Box 9818
Birmingham
B11 4WA
United Kingdom
www.Daarussunnah.com
e-mail: info@Daarussunnah.com
Tel/Fax: +44 0 121 766 7993

British Library Cataloguing in publication Data.
A catalogue record for this book is available from the British Library.

ISBN 1-904336-11-6
Paper-back

Published by: Daar us-Sunnah Publishers
Typeset by: Daar us-Sunnah Publishers
Cover design for: Daar us-Sunnah Publishers
First Edition, 1424 AH/2004 CE

Contents

Transliteration Table

Consonants. Arabic

initial: unexpressed medial and final:

ء '	د d	ض ḍ	ك k
ب b	ذ dh	ط ṭ	ل l
ت t	ر r	ظ ẓ	م m
ث th	ز z	ع ʿ	ن n
ج j	س s	غ gh	هـ h
ح ḥ	ش sh	ف f	و w
خ kh	ص ṣ	ق q	ي y

Vowels, diphthongs, etc.

Short:	ـَ a	ـِ i	ـُ u
long:	ـَا ā	ـُو ū	ـِي ī

Biography of the Author

He is Abū Muḥammad ʿIzz ad-Dīn ʿAbdu-l-ʿAzīz bin ʿAbdu-s-Salām bin Abū al-Qāsim bin al-Ḥasan bin Muḥammad bin al-Muhadhdhab as-Sulamī ash-Shāfiʿī, nicknamed the Sulṭān of the scholars. He was born in Damascus in the year 577 or 578H to a poor family.

Not much is known of his childhood or upbringing but it is known that he studied under the scholars of Damascus and then travelled to Baghdad for a short time, studying under its scholars. The first of his teachers was the judge, Jamāl ad-Dīn al-Harastānī and Abū Ṭāhir Barakāt al-Khushūʿī, the famous Ḥāfiẓ, under whom he studied ḥadīth. Then he began to attend the lessons of Fakhr ad-Dīn ibn ʿAsākir, the Imām of the Shāfiʿīs in Shām, and learnt fiqh from him. He studied the fundaments of usūl al-fiqh with Ṣayf ad-Dīn al-Āmidī, the famous expert in this field and progressed his studies of ḥadīth under Bahāʾ ad-Dīn ibn ʿAsākir, the famous scholar of ḥadīth. He acquired a thorough knowledge of the various Islāmic sciences and attained the level of mujtahid.

The author also delivered sermons, presented lectures and taught and did so until he passed away, teaching in a number of the famous schools of Damascus and then in Cairo. He was firm against innovation and eradicated many innovations that were current in his day. He always spoke the truth, even if it be against the rulers and when the ruler of Damascus gave away some land to the Franks, he stopped supplicating for him from the pulpit. As a result he was imprisoned, then ultimately exiled to Egypt. In Egypt, he directly addressed its ruler in front of his army, demanding that he eradicate the evils that were being practiced there such as the drinking of wine and these practices were put to an end. When asked if he had been afraid, he replied by saying that he brought to mind the greatness of Allāh and it seemed as of the ruler had become like a kitten.

Aside from his courage, he was also known for his piety and asceticism, and when he moved to Egypt, he quickly became the leading religious authority, with legal verdicts being deferred to him.

He had many students, amongst whom were: ibn Daqīq al-'Īd, Shihāb ad-Dīn al-Qarāfī, 'Alā' ad-Dīn al-Bājī, Sharaf ad-Dīn ad-Dimyāṭī and ibn al-Munayyir.

He authored many works, from amongst which were: *Tafsīr al-Qur'ān, al-Fawā'id fī Mushkil al-Qur'ān, Majāz al-Qur'ān, Mukhtaṣar Ṣaḥīḥ Muslim, al-'Aqā'id, al-Farq bayn al-Īmān wa-l-Islām, Qawā'id al-Aḥkām, al-Qawā'id as-Ṣughrā, al-Imām fī Bayān Adillah al-Aḥkām, Fatāwā al-Miṣriyyah, Shajaratu-l-Ma'ārif, Sharḥ Asmā' al-Ḥusnā* and *Bidāyatu-s-Sūl fī Tafḍīl ar-Rasūl.*

He passed away in Egypt in the year 660H at the age of eighty-two or eighty-three, may Allāh have mercy upon him.

Trials and Tribulations
Wisdom and Benefits

With the Name of Allāh, the All-Merciful, the Most Merciful
Peace and Blessings be upon our master, Muḥammad, his family and his Companions

The Shaykh, the Imām, the Proof of Islām, Abū Muḥammad ʿAbdu-l-ʿAzīz bin ʿAbdu-s-Salām bin Abū al-Qāsim as-Sulamī ash-Shāfiʿī, may Allāh benefit the Muslims through him and forgive him, us and all the Muslims, said:

In tribulations, trials, misfortunes and calamities lie a number of benefits; these benefits have differing degrees of relevance, differing in accordance to the various ranks of people.

• Realising the greatness of Allāh's Lordship and His all-encompassing power.

• Realising the humility and dejection of servitude. It is to this that the saying of Allāh, Exalted is He, points to,

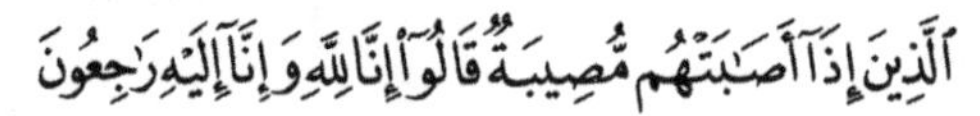

«Those who, when disaster strikes them, say, 'we belong to Allāh and to Him will we return'»
[*al-Baqarah* (2): 156]

They acknowledge that they belong to Him, that they are but lowly servants of His, that they will return to Him for judgment and are subject to His decree and regulation. They know that they have nowhere to flee from Him and no way to escape Him.

• Actualising sincerity for Allāh, Exalted is He. This is because there is no way to repress hardship except by recoursing to Him and there is no one that one can depend on to remove it except Him,

وَإِن يَمْسَسْكَ ٱللَّهُ بِضُرٍّ فَلَا كَاشِفَ لَهُۥٓ إِلَّا هُوَ

«If Allāh touches you with harm, none can remove it but Him...»

[*al-An'ām* (6): 17]

فَإِذَا رَكِبُوا۟ فِى ٱلْفُلْكِ دَعَوُا۟ ٱللَّهَ مُخْلِصِينَ لَهُ ٱلدِّينَ

«When they embark on ships, they call on Allāh, making their religion sincerely His...»

[*al-'Ankābūt* (29): 65]

• Turning in penitence[1] to Allāh, Exalted is He, and directing ones heart to Him,

وَإِذَا مَسَّ ٱلْإِنسَـٰنَ ضُرٌّ دَعَا رَبَّهُۥ مُنِيبًا إِلَيْهِ

«When harm touches man he calls upon his Lord, turning in repentance to Him»

[*az-Zumar* (39): 8]

---

[1] *Inābah*: returning. ibn al-Qayyim, *Madārij as-Sālikīn* [1/467] said, '*inābah* comprises four matters: the love of Allāh, submission to Him, turning to Him, and turning away from everything besides Him. A person cannot be said to "penitent" unless he meets all four requirements and the explanation of the Salaf to this word revolves around this. The word also carries the meaning of quickness, returning and precedence; therefore the penitent is rushing to do that which would please his Lord, turning back to Him at every moment and foremost in doing that which He loves.'

- Submissiveness and supplication,[2]

فَإِذَا مَسَّ ٱلْإِنسَٰنَ ضُرٌّ دَعَانَا

«When harm touches man he calls on Us...»

[*az-Zumar* (39): 49]

وَإِذَا مَسَّكُمُ ٱلضُّرُّ فِي ٱلْبَحْرِ ضَلَّ مَن تَدْعُونَ إِلَّآ إِيَّاهُ

«When harm touches you at sea, those you call on vanish - except for Him alone!»

[*al-Isrā'* (17): 67]

بَلْ إِيَّاهُ تَدْعُونَ فَيَكْشِفُ مَا تَدْعُونَ إِلَيْهِ إِن شَآءَ وَتَنسَوْنَ مَا تُشْرِكُونَ ﴿٤١﴾

«It is Him you call on and, if He wills, He will deliver you from whatever it was that made you call on Him...»

[*al-An'ām* (6): 41]

قُلْ مَن يُنَجِّيكُم مِّن ظُلُمَٰتِ ٱلْبَرِّ وَٱلْبَحْرِ تَدْعُونَهُۥ تَضَرُّعًا وَخُفْيَةً لَّئِنْ أَنجَىٰنَا مِنْ هَٰذِهِۦ لَنَكُونَنَّ مِنَ ٱلشَّٰكِرِينَ ﴿٦٣﴾ قُلِ ٱللَّهُ يُنَجِّيكُم مِّنْهَا وَمِن كُلِّ كَرْبٍ ثُمَّ أَنتُمْ تُشْرِكُونَ ﴿٦٤﴾

«Say: 'who rescues you from the darkness of the land and sea? You call on Him humbly and secretly:...' Say: 'Allāh rescues you from it and

---

[2] *Du'ā*: to call out, to summon. al-Khaṭṭābī, *Sha'n ad-Du'ā* [p. 4] said, 'the meaning of du'ā is the servants asking his Lord for His help and continued support. Its essence is that a person shows his need of Allāh and expresses his inability to change any matter himself or having any power and ability. This characteristic is the mark of servitude and exemplifies it. *Du'ā* also carries with it the meaning of praising Allāh and attributing to Him generosity and grace.'

from every plight, then you associate others with Him!'»

[*al-An'ām* (6): 63-64]

- Forbearance,[3]

إِنَّ إِبْرَٰهِيمَ لَأَوَّٰهٌ حَلِيمٌ

«Ibrāhīm was tender-hearted and forbearing»

[*at-Tawbah* (9): 114]

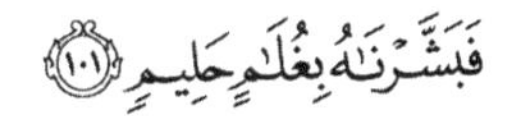

«...and We gave give glad-tidings of a forbearing boy»

[*as-Ṣāffāt* (37): 101]

---

[3] *Ḥilm*: the abandonment of haste. ar-Rāghib, *al-Mufradāt* said, 'it is the ability to control the soul and temperament at the onrush of anger.' al-Jāhiẓ, *Tahdhīb al-Akhlāq* said, 'it is the abandonment of taking revenge in the state of extreme anger, despite the ability to do so.' al-Jurjāni, *at-Ta'rīfāt* said, 'it is to be calm in the state of anger.'

ibn Ḥibbān (d. 354H), *Rawḍatu-l-'Uqalā'* [pp. 170-174] said, 'it is to prevent the soul, at the onset of something that it dislikes, from falling into that which is prohibited. It is made up of cognisance (*ma'rifah*), patience (*ṣabr*), deliberation (*anāh*) and examination and circumspection (*tathabbut*). ...Were *ḥilm* to have no praiseworthy trait except preventing one from falling into sin and entering into despicable situations, this would be sufficient in making it obligatory upon the intelligent to adhere to whenever he finds the opportunity...It is obligatory upon the intelligent when he becomes angry and exasperated to bring to mind the *ḥilm* that Allāh displays to him despite his frequently transgressing the bounds and falling into sin, this should then direct him to showing *ḥilm* and prevent his anger from leading to sin...were *ḥilm* to have parents, one of them would be intelligence and the other silence.'

al-Māwardī (d.450H), *Adab ad-Dunyā wa-d-Dīn* [p. 184] said, '*ḥilm* is from the most noble of qualities and the most deserving of being possessed by the intelligent, the perspicuous. It serves to preserve ones honour, keep one free from trouble and worry, and attract respect and praise.'

The Prophet (ﷺ) said [to Ashaj 'Abdu-l-Qays],

> You have two qualities that Allāh loves: forbearance and deliberation[4]

The ranking of forbearance differs in accordance to the magnitude of calamity; showing forbearance at the onset of the severest calamities is from its greatest manifestations.

- Forgiving the human agent who caused the trial,

وَٱلْعَافِينَ عَنِ ٱلنَّاسِ

«...those who pardon others...»

[*Āli 'Imrān* (3): 134]

فَمَنْ عَفَا وَأَصْلَحَ فَأَجْرُهُۥ عَلَى ٱللَّهِ

«...but if someone pardons and puts things right, his reward is with Allāh»

[*ash-Shūrā* (42): 40]

Showing forgiveness at the onset of the greatest of calamities is from its greatest manifestations.[5]

---

[4] Muslim [#17, 18] on the authority of ibn 'Abbās and Abū Sa'īd al-Khudrī

[5] ibn Ḥibbān [p. 131] said, 'it is necessary that the intelligent accustom his soul to forgiving people and to leave repaying evil with evil. This is because there is nothing that would silence an evil better than good treatment and beneficence and there is nothing that would stir up evil more than repaying evil with evil... Whoever desires copious reward, to receive devout love and good mention, let him experience the bitterness of opposing his base desires and taking to the way we have highlighted: joining relations when they have been severed; giving in the face of prevention; *ḥilm* in the face of ignorance; and forgiveness in the face of oppression. These are the greatest morals and manners of the religious.'

• Patience and steadfastness in the face of affliction,[6] this leads to Allāh's love and increase in His rewards,

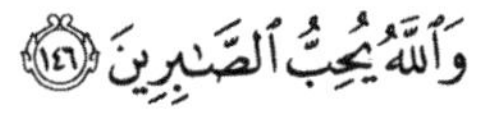

«...Allāh loves the patient and steadfast...»
[*Āli 'Imrān* (3): 146]

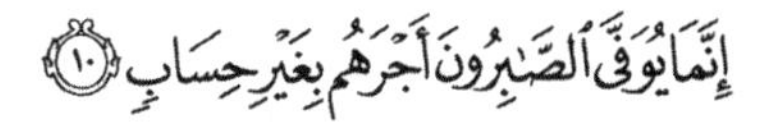

«The patient and steadfast will be repaid their wages in full without any reckoning»
[*az-Zumar* (39): 10]

The Messenger of Allāh (ﷺ) said,

> None has been given a gift better and more encompassing than patience.[7]

---

[6] *Ṣabr*: to refrain and withhold. ar-Rāghib said, 'it is to withhold the soul as determined by the Legal Law and the intellect.' al-Jāḥiẓ said that it is a quality made up of sobriety and courage and al-Manāwī said that it was the ability to face disturbing and painful circumstances, both physical and mental. It is to withhold the soul from misery and displeasure, the tongue from complaining and the limbs from derangement; it is to remain firm upon the laws of Allāh in all circumstances and to face adversity with the best of conduct.

ibn Ḥibbān [pp. 126-128] said, 'it is obligatory upon the intelligent, in the beginning, to adhere firmly to *ṣabr* at the onset of difficulty. When he becomes firm in this he should then move on to the level of contentment (*riḍā*). If one has not been nourished with *ṣabr* he should adhere firmly to inculcating *ṣabr* in himself (*taṣabbur*) for that is the first stages of *riḍā*. If a man was to have *ṣabr*, truly would he be noble; for *ṣabr* is the fount of all good and the foundation of all obedience... The stages leading to it are concern (*ihtimām*), awakening (*tayakkuẓ*), examination and circumspection (*tathabbut*), and *taṣabbur*, after it comes *riḍā* and that is the peak of the spiritual stations... *ṣabr* is displayed in three matters: *ṣabr* from sin; *ṣābr* upon obedience; and *ṣabr* at the face of adversity and calamity.' See also ibn al-Qayyim, *Madārij as-Sālikīn* [1/162-165]

[7] Bukhārī [#1429] and Muslim [#1053] on the authority of Abū Sa'īd al-Khudrī

• Experiencing joy at the onset of calamity because of the many benefits it contains. The Messenger of Allāh (ﷺ) said,

> By the One in whose hand is my soul, they [the righteous] would show joy at the onset of calamity as you show joy in times of ease.[8]

Ibn Mas'ūd (*raḍiyAllāhu 'anhu*) said, 'truly amazing are the two detested ones: death and poverty!'[9] They showed joy at the onset of calamity because they knew full well that there is no comparison between its hardship and its fruits and benefits. This situation is comparable to one who is cured from severe illness after drinking foul medicine.[10]

---

[8] ibn Mājah [#4024] on the authority of Abū Sa'īd al-Khudrī. al-Būṣayrī said its isnād was ṣaḥīḥ as did al-Ḥākim [#119] with adh-Dhahabī agreeing as did al-Albānī, *as-Ṣaḥīḥah* [#144]

[9] Abū Nu'aym, *al-Ḥilyah* [1/180 #416]

[10] Abū Umāmah reports that the Messenger of Allāh (ﷺ) said, "Allāh tests you through tribulation in order to refine you, just as you refine gold with fire. Amongst you are those who are left resembling pure gold - such is a person whom Allāh has saved from evil deeds; amongst you are those who are left resembling gold of lesser quality - such is a person who falls into some degree of doubt; and amongst you are those who are left resembling black gold - such a person is one who gives in to the trial."

Recorded by al-Bayhaqī, *Shu'ab* [#9924] and al-Ḥākim [#7878] said it was ṣaḥīḥ with adh-Dhahabī agreeing.

'Alī (*raḍiyAllāhu 'anhu*) said, 'son of Ādam! Do not rejoice at wealth and do not despair at poverty. Do not become despondent at the onset of tribulation and do not rejoice at the onset of ease for gold is refined through fire and the righteous servant is refined through tribulation. You will not attain what you want except be leaving what you desire and you will not reach what you aspire to except through *ṣabr*. Expend all your efforts in carefully fulfilling the duties made obligatory upon you.'

• Being grateful[11] at the onset of calamity because of the many benefits it contains. Comparable to this is the case of a sick person thanking a doctor who has just amputated one of his limbs in order to save his life, even though this would serve to disable him to some extent.

• Its expiating sins and errors,

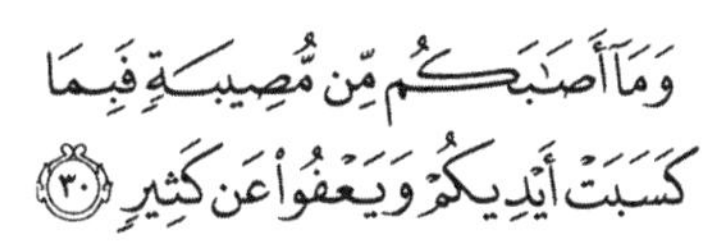

«Any disaster that strikes you is through what your own hands have earned and He pardons much»

[*ash-Shūrā* (42): 30]

The Messenger of Allāh (ﷺ) said,

The believer is not afflicted with illness or hardship, even if it be a worry that troubles him or a thorn

[11] *Shukr*: praising another for the good that he has done to one. Ibn al-Qayyim [2/244] said, '*shukr* is to display the effects of the blessings of Allāh upon the tongue by way of praise and acknowledgment; in the heart by way of witnessing and love; and upon the limbs by way of submission and obedience.' al-Fairozabādī said that *shukr* was built upon five pillars: submission to the One who gave the blessings; loving Him; acknowledging His blessing; praising Him for it; and not using it in any way that may displease Him.

Ibn Ḥajr, *Fatḥ al-Bārī* [11/311] said, '*shukr* comprises *ṣabr* upon obedience and away from disobedience. Some of the Imāms said that *ṣabr* necessitates *shukr* and cannot be completed without it, and the opposite; hence if one of them goes so too does the other. So whoever is in a state of receiving favours, it is obligatory upon him to show *ṣabr* and *shukr*, *ṣabr* from disobedience. Whoever is in a state of trial, it is also obligatory upon him to show *ṣabr* and *shukr*, *shukr* by establishing the rights of Allāh during that trial. Indeed servitude is due to Allāh in times of tribulation and in times of ease.'

> that pricks him, except that his sins would be expiated as a result of it.[12]

• Showing mercy to those who are undergoing affliction and coming to their aid. [It is reported that ʿĪsā (ﷺ) would say],

> People are either living in times of ease and well-being or facing tribulation, so be merciful to those who are facing tribulation and thank Allāh for your own well-being.[13]

[The poet said],

The only one to show mercy upon the lovers is one who has loved

• Understanding the greatness of the blessing of ease and well-being. This is because blessings are never truly appreciated until one loses them.

• Understanding what Allāh, Exalted is He, has caused to be the outcome of these benefits in terms of reward in the Hereafter.

• Realising the many hidden benefits it contains,

فَعَسَىٰٓ أَن تَكْرَهُوا۟ شَيْـًٔا وَيَجْعَلَ ٱللَّهُ فِيهِ خَيْرًا كَثِيرًا ﴿١٩﴾

«...it may well be that you dislike something in which Allāh has placed a lot of good»

[*an-Nisā'* (4): 19]

---

[12] Bukhārī [#5641] and Muslim [#2573]

[13] Mālik [2/986]

وَعَسَىٰٓ أَن تَكْرَهُوا۟ شَيْـًٔا وَهُوَ خَيْرٌ لَّكُمْ

«...it may be that you hate something when it is good for you...»

[*al-Baqarah* (2): 216]

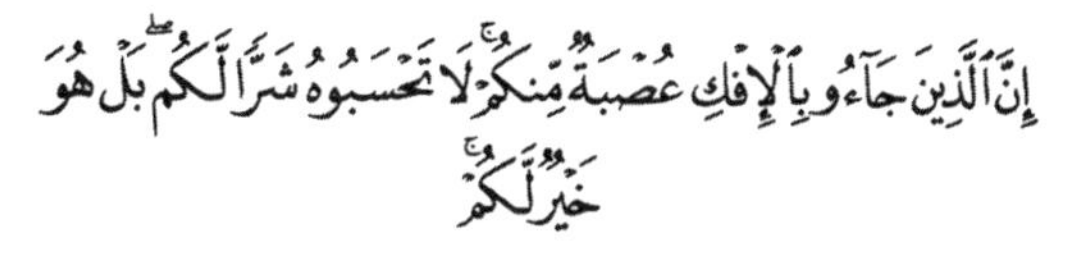

«Those who propagated the lie, do not suppose it to be bad for you; rather it is good for you»

[*an-Nūr* (24): 11]

When the tyrannical ruler took Sārah from Ibrāhīm, one of the hidden benefits of this trial was that later she was given Hājar as a servant who bore Ibrāhīm, Ismā'īl, from whose progeny was born the Master of the Messengers and the Seal of the Prophets (ﷺ). Look and see how great the hidden benefit was in that trial! It is said,

How many are the blessings hidden
Under the veil of tribulations

Another person said,

Perhaps something that is detested, hateful
Contains much blessings from Allāh

- Tribulation and hardship prevents one from evil, vanity, boastfulness, arrogance, ostentation and oppression. Were Nimrod someone poor and feeble, blind and deaf, he would never have argued with Ibrāhīm concerning his Lord; however he was deceived into this by his sovereignty as pointed out by Allāh, Exalted is He,

أَلَمْ تَرَ إِلَى ٱلَّذِى حَآجَّ إِبْرَٰهِـۧمَ فِى رَبِّهِۦٓ أَنْ ءَاتَىٰهُ ٱللَّهُ ٱلْمُلْكَ

«What about the one who argued with Ibrāhīm about his Lord, on the basis that Allāh had given him sovereignty?»

[*al-Baqarah* (2): 258]

Were Pharaoh to have been similarly tried, he would never have said,

فَقَالَ أَنَا۠ رَبُّكُمُ ٱلْأَعْلَىٰ ﴿٢٤﴾

«I am your Lord Most High!»

[*an-Nāzi'āt* (79): 24]

Allāh, Exalted is He, says,

وَمَا نَقَمُوٓا۟ إِلَّآ أَنْ أَغْنَىٰهُمُ ٱللَّهُ وَرَسُولُهُۥ مِن فَضْلِهِۦ

«...they were vindictive for no cause other than that Allāh and His Messenger had enriched them from His bounty»

[*at-Tawbah* (9): 74]

كَلَّآ إِنَّ ٱلْإِنسَـٰنَ لَيَطْغَىٰٓ ﴿٦﴾ أَن رَّءَاهُ ٱسْتَغْنَىٰٓ ﴿٧﴾

«No indeed! Truly man is unbridled, seeing himself as self-sufficient»

[*al-'Alaq* (96): 6-7]

وَلَوْ بَسَطَ ٱللَّهُ ٱلرِّزْقَ لِعِبَادِهِۦ لَبَغَوْا۟ فِى ٱلْأَرْضِ

«Were Allāh to expand the provision of His servants, they would act as tyrants on the earth»

[*ash-Shūrā* (42): 27]

وَاتَّبَعَ الَّذِينَ
ظَلَمُوا مَا أُتْرِفُوا فِيهِ وَكَانُوا مُجْرِمِينَ ﴿١١٦﴾

«Those who did wrong gladly pursued the life of luxury that they were given...»

[*Hūd* (11): 116]

لَأَسْقَيْنَاهُم مَّاءً غَدَقًا ﴿١٦﴾ لِّنَفْتِنَهُمْ فِيهِ

«...We would give them abundant water so that We could test them by it»

[*al-Jinn* (72): 16-17]

وَمَا أَرْسَلْنَا فِي قَرْيَةٍ
مِّن نَّذِيرٍ إِلَّا قَالَ مُتْرَفُوهَا إِنَّا بِمَا أُرْسِلْتُم بِهِ كَافِرُونَ ﴿٣٤﴾

«We never sent a warner into any city without the affluent people saying, 'we reject what you have been sent with'»

[*Saba'* (34): 34]

It is because of these great benefits that those who were tried most severely were the Prophets, then the righteous and then those closest to them.[14] They were accused of being mad, magicians, fortune tellers; they were mocked and ridiculed,

فَصَبَرُوا عَلَىٰ مَا كُذِّبُوا وَأُوذُوا

«...but they were steadfast in the face of denial and injury they suffered...»

[*al-An'ām* (6): 34]

---

[14] Aḥmad [#1481, 1494, 1555, 1607], at-Tirmidhī [#2400] and ibn Mājah [#4023] on the authority of Sa'd bin Abī Waqqāṣ. at-Tirmidhī said it was ḥasan ṣaḥīḥ; al-Ḥākim [#120] said it was ṣaḥīḥ and adh-Dhahabī agreed.

It has been said to us,

أَمْ حَسِبْتُمْ أَن تَدْخُلُوا۟ ٱلْجَنَّةَ وَلَمَّا
يَأْتِكُم مَّثَلُ ٱلَّذِينَ خَلَوْا۟ مِن قَبْلِكُم ۖ مَّسَّتْهُمُ ٱلْبَأْسَآءُ وَٱلضَّرَّآءُ
وَزُلْزِلُوا۟ حَتَّىٰ يَقُولَ ٱلرَّسُولُ وَٱلَّذِينَ ءَامَنُوا۟ مَعَهُۥ مَتَىٰ نَصْرُ ٱللَّهِ ۗ
أَلَآ إِنَّ نَصْرَ ٱللَّهِ قَرِيبٌ ﴿٢١٤﴾

«Or do you suppose that you would enter Paradise without facing the same as those who came before you? Poverty and illness afflicted them and they were shaken to the point that the Prophet and the believers with him said, 'when is Allāh's help coming?' Be assured that Allāh's help is very near»

[*al-Baqarah* (2): 214]

وَلَنَبْلُوَنَّكُم بِشَىْءٍ مِّنَ ٱلْخَوْفِ وَٱلْجُوعِ
وَنَقْصٍ مِّنَ ٱلْأَمْوَٰلِ وَٱلْأَنفُسِ وَٱلثَّمَرَٰتِ ۗ وَبَشِّرِ ٱلصَّٰبِرِينَ

«We will test you with a certain amount of fear and hunger and loss of wealth, life and fruits. But give good news to the steadfast...»

[*al-Baqarah* (2): 155]

لَتُبْلَوُنَّ فِىٓ أَمْوَٰلِكُمْ
وَأَنفُسِكُمْ وَلَتَسْمَعُنَّ مِنَ ٱلَّذِينَ أُوتُوا۟ ٱلْكِتَٰبَ
مِن قَبْلِكُمْ وَمِنَ ٱلَّذِينَ أَشْرَكُوٓا۟

«You will be tested in your wealth and in yourselves and you will hear many abusive words from those who were given the Book before you and from the polytheists»

[*Āli 'Imrān* (3): 186]

The Companions were evicted from their homes and lands, forced to flee leaving their possessions behind them, their tribulations went from severity to severity, their enemies multiplied in number, on occasion they were overcome and defeated, many of them were killed at Uḥud and other places and battles, the Messenger of Allāh (ﷺ) received injury in his face, one of his molar teeth was broken and his helmet was crushed into the sides of his head and split to expose his head; his enemies rejoiced and his associates despaired. On the Day of al-Khandaq they were tried to the point that,

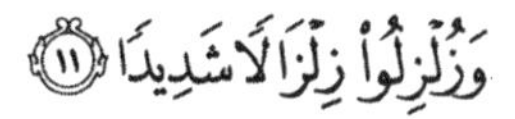

«...the believers were tested and severely shaken»

[*al-Aḥzāb* (33): 11]

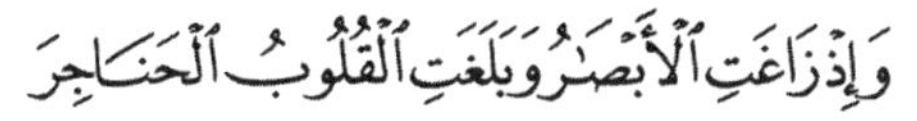

«...when the eyes rolled and the hearts rose to the throats...»

[*al-Aḥzāb* (33): 10]

They would live in a constant state of fear, destitution and poverty. They would be forced to tie rocks to their stomachs out of severe hunger and the Master of the first and last never ate his fill of bread twice in any one day.[15] He was injured in various ways to the point that they accused the chastity of his most beloved wife. Then, towards the end of his life, he was tried with Musaylamah, Ṭulayḥah and al-'Ansī.[16] When he (ﷺ)

---

[15] Muslim [#2970]

[16] These were all people who claimed Prophethood.

passed away, his armour was mortgaged to a Jew for thirty sāʿ of wheat.[17]

The Prophets and righteous have always faced trials and tribulations, with each person being tried in proportion to his religion. Some of them would be sawn in half but this would not make them renegade from their faith. The Messenger of Allāh (ﷺ) said,

> The example of the believer is like that of a plant, the wind is always making it lean in one direction and then another, in the same way the believer is always afflicted with trial.[18]

> The example of the believer is like the stem of a fresh tender plant, the wind causing it bend sometimes, fall over sometimes and stand erect at others until it withers and dies.[19]

The state of hardship and tribulation causes the servant to turn towards Allāh, Mighty and Magnificent.[20] The state of ease,

---

[17] Bukhārī [#2916] on the authority of ʿĀ'ishah

[18] Bukhārī [#5644] and Muslim [#2809] on the authority of Abū Hurayrah

[19] Bukhārī [#5643] and Muslim [#2810] on the authority of Kaʿb bin Mālik

[20] al-Manāwī, *Fayḍ al-Qadīr* [1/245] said, 'al-Ghazālī said, "if you see Allāh, Mighty and Magnificent, holding back this world from you, frequently trying you with adversity and tribulation, know that you hold a great status with Him. Know that He is dealing with you as he does with His Awliyā' and chosen elite and is watching over you, have you not heard His saying,

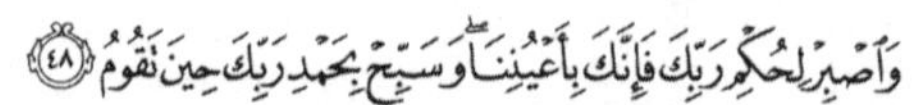

«so wait steadfastly for the judgment of your Lord - you

well-being and blessings causes the servant to turn away from Allāh, Exalted is He,

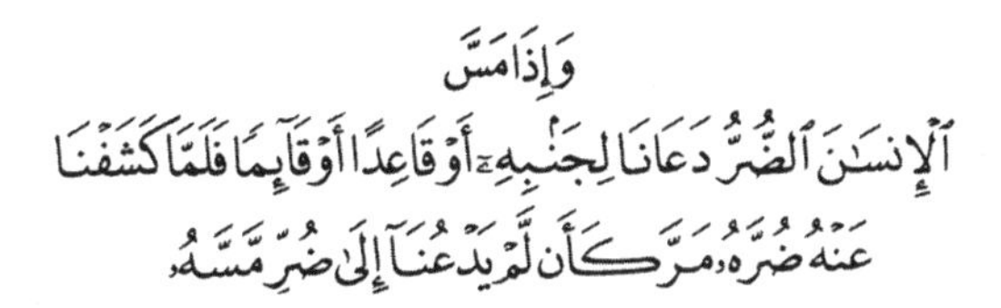

«When harm touches man, he calls on Us, lying on his side or sitting down or standing up. Then when We remove the harm from him he carries on as if he had never called on Us when the harm first touched him»

[*Yūnus (*10): 12]

This is why they ate scarcely and wore modest clothing etc. so that they could be in a state that would lead them to turn back to Allāh, Mighty and Magnificent, and devote themselves to Him.

- Being pleased and content[21] with the tribulation such that it

---

are certainly before Our eyes»

[*at-Ṭūr* (52): 48],

so acknowledge this great favour upon you." '

[21] *Riḍā*: the opposite of displeasure and malcontent. al-Jurjānī said that it referred to the joy of the heart at the occurrence of the decree. Ibn al-Qayyim [2/185] mentioned that it is the tranquillity of the heart in the face of the vicissitudes of the decree and the firm knowledge that it has that Allāh would only that which is good for it.

ibn Rajab, *Jāmiʿ al-ʿUlūm wa-l-Ḥikam* [1/239] said, '*riḍā* is recommended whereas *ṣabr* is obligatory, from *ṣabr* ensues a great deal of good... The difference between *riḍā* and *ṣabr* is that *ṣabr* is to restrain ones soul from feeling and displaying displeasure or malcontent coupled with sensing the pain of what has befallen him and the desire to see it removed; *riḍā* is the expansion of the would lead to the pleasure of Allāh, Exalted is He. This is because both the righteous and sinner is afflicted with trial, hence whoever is malcontent at its onset, for him is displeasure and misery in this life and the Hereafter. Whoever is pleased and content with it, for him lies in store the good pleasure of Allāh and that is greater than Paradise and what it contains, for Allāh, Exalted is He, says,

«...and Allāh's good pleasure is even greater»
[*at-Tawbah* (9): 72]

i.e. greater than the Gardens of Paradise.

These are brief perusals into what comes to mind concerning the benefits of tribulation. We ask Allāh that He forgive us and give us well-being in this world and the Hereafter. May Allāh grants us the accord to enact that which He loves and is pleased with. Peace and blessings be upon Muḥammad, his family and Companions. Allāh is sufficient for us and what an excellent disposer of our affairs is He.

---

heart to what has befallen it, its total acceptance of the divine decree and its not desiring to see it removed. Even though one may feel pain, *riḍā* lessens that pain because of the certainty (*yaqīn*) and cognisance (*maʿrifah*) that has taken root in the heart. As the state of *riḍā* strengthens it is even possible that the person no longer feel the pain at all.'

al-Bayhaqī [#209] records that ibn Masʿūd (*raḍiyAllāhu ʿanhu*) said, '*riḍā* is that you not please the people at the expense of the displeasure of Allāh; that you not praise anyone for the provision Allāh has granted you; and that you not blame anyone for that which Allāh has not given you. The grant of provision is not dictated by the desire of a person and neither is it withheld because of the dislike of another. It is Allāh, through His knowledge and justice, Who has placed relief and joy in certainty and *riḍā* and placed worry and despair in doubt and malcontent.'

APPENDIX

Trials and Tribulations
Wisdom and Benefits

Shaykh al-Islām, al-Ḥāfiẓ ibn al-Qayyim said:[1]

Complete felicity is to be found in the True Religion, by implementing it in speech and deed. Those who follow this religion are the one who attains this felicity as Allāh, Exalted is He, says,

ٱهْدِنَا ٱلصِّرَٰطَ ٱلْمُسْتَقِيمَ ﴿٦﴾ صِرَٰطَ ٱلَّذِينَ أَنْعَمْتَ
عَلَيْهِمْ غَيْرِ ٱلْمَغْضُوبِ عَلَيْهِمْ وَلَا ٱلضَّآلِّينَ ﴿٧﴾

«Guide us to the Straight Path; the path of those whom You have favoured; not [the path] of those whose portion is anger nor those who have gone astray»

[*al-Fātiḥah* (1): 6-7]

أُو۟لَٰٓئِكَ عَلَىٰ هُدًى مِّن رَّبِّهِمْ ۖ وَأُو۟لَٰٓئِكَ هُمُ ٱلْمُفْلِحُونَ ﴿٥﴾

«...They are the people guided by their Lord, they are the successful»

[*al-Baqarah* (2): 5]

فَإِمَّا يَأْتِيَنَّكُم مِّنِّى هُدًى
فَمَنِ ٱتَّبَعَ هُدَاىَ فَلَا يَضِلُّ وَلَا يَشْقَىٰ ﴿١٢٣﴾

---

[1] ibn al-Qayyim, *Ighāthatu-l-Lahfān min Maṣāyidi-sh-Shayṭān* [2/254-281]

«...and if there should come to you guidance from Me - whoever follows My guidance will neither go astray nor suffer»

[*Ṭā Ḥā* (20): 123]

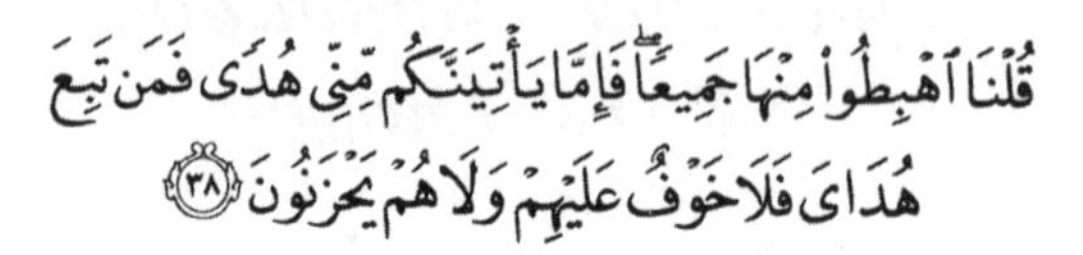

«...and when guidance comes to You from Me, whoever follows My guidance - there will be no fear concerning them, nor will they grieve»

[*al-Baqarah* (2): 38]

«The truly good will be in perfect Bliss and the dissolute will be in a Blazing Fire»

[*al-Infiṭār* (82): 13-14]

The promise that the followers of guidance and righteous deeds will be in perfect Bliss in the Hereafter, the threat that the disbelievers and sinners will be in torment in the Hereafter, is something that all the Messengers have agreed upon. However we shall mention a beneficial point here:

People often see, and hear of, the believers being afflicted with adversity and tribulation, and conversely they often see, and hear of, the disbelievers attaining leadership and wealth in this world. This leads them to believe that well-being in this world is only reserved for the disbelievers and only a fraction of it is given to the believers; and also to believe that nobility and might is for the disbelievers in this world and for the believers in the Hereafter. When such a person, who believes in the truth of the Qur'ān, hears verses such as,

وَلِلَّهِ ٱلْعِزَّةُ وَلِرَسُولِهِۦ وَلِلْمُؤْمِنِينَ

«...but all might belongs to Allāh and to His Messenger and to the believers»

[*al-Munāfiqūn* (63): 8]

«It is Our army which will be victorious»

[*as-Ṣaffāt* (37): 173]

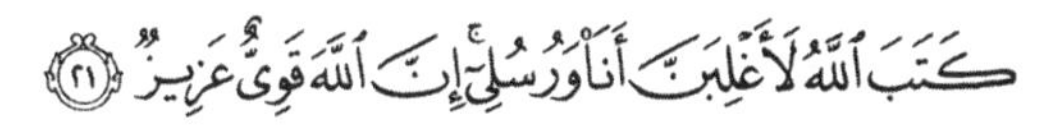

«Allāh has decreed, 'I will be victorious, I and My Messengers'...»

[*al-Mujādilah* (58): 21]

وَٱلْعَٰقِبَةُ لِلْمُتَّقِينَ

«The successful outcome is for those who have taqwā»

[*al-A'rāf* (7): 128][2]

he believes that they refer to the Hereafter only and this belief is further strengthened when he sees the disbelievers and hypocrites vanquishing and subjugating the Muslims. If such a person is asked why Allāh would allow this to happen to his Awliyā', his beloved friends, those who follow the truth, he will

[2] Ibn Taymiyyah, *Majmū' Fatāwā* [10/433] says, '*taqwā* is that the person act in obedience to Allāh upon a light from Him and that he abandon disobedience to Him upon a light from Him, fearing the punishment of Allāh.'

He also says, *Majmū' Rasā'il* [1/256], '*taqwā* in actions comes about by meeting two requirements, the first that the deed be sincerely for Allāh; meaning by this that one desire only the Face of Allāh and not associate anything else in the worship of his Lord, the second that the deed be something Allāh has commanded and loves, i.e. it be in conformity to the Legal Law and not in accordance to some other law that Allāh has not allowed to be followed.'

reply in one of two ways. If he is of those who do not believe that the Actions of Allāh arise from wisdom and benefit, he will reply by saying that Allāh does what He wills,

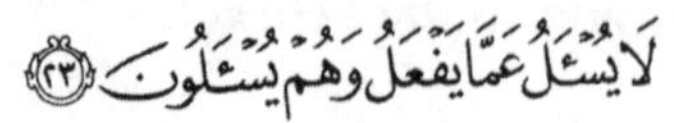

«He will not be questioned about what He does, but they will be questioned»

[*al-Anbiyā*ʾ (21): 23]

If, on the other hand, he does believe that the actions of Allāh are dictated by wisdom and benefit, he will reply by saying that this happens so that they may actualise *ṣabr* and attain the reward of the Hereafter, reward without measure that is meted out to the patient, along with achieving exalted ranking.

Both these groups go on to address various issues, problems and queries concerning their belief, answering them in accordance to the level of their cognisance, or ignorance as the case may be, of Allāh, His Names and Attributes, many times causing the heart to boil in horror at what they say! We have witnessed many incidents from these people, and other cases have been conveyed to us, whereby they end up accusing the Lord, Exalted is He, of plain oppression and other things that could only arise from an enemy of Allāh! al-Jahm used to go out with his followers to lepers and people facing adversity and say, 'look at them! Could the Most Merciful of the merciful do this?' intending thereby to reject the Attribute of mercy just as he had rejected the Attribute of wisdom. Another person used to say, 'there is no one who harms the creation more than the Creator.' Yet another said in a line of poetry,

If this is what He does to His beloved
What can one expect Him to do to His enemies?

We see many people who face trial and tribulation crying out, 'my Lord! What sin have I done for You to do this to me!'

More than one person has said to me, 'when I repent to Him and work righteous deeds, He restricts my provision and makes life difficult. When I return to sin and submit to my lusts, provision and ease come freely to me.' I say to them, 'this is a test from Allāh so that He may see your truthfulness and patience. Are you truthful in turning to Him and going to Him, are you able to bear His trial with patience so that the end will be for you; or are you untruthful in your repentance.'

These false thoughts and statements are built upon two foundations:

The first: the servants thinking well of himself and his religious practice, his believing that he has fulfilled what is obligatory upon him to do and leave what is prohibited for him to do; all of this coupled with the belief that his enemy or opponent has not done this, believing that he himself is more deserving of Allāh and His Messenger than he.

The second: his belief that Allāh, Glorious is He, could quite possibly not aid the follower of the True Religion and not appoint for him any sort of success in this world, instead having him live a life of subjugation and oppression, this despite his establishing what Allāh has commanded of him; inwardly and outwardly.

There is none worthy of worship besides Allāh! How many ignorant servants, how many devout people with no insight, how many people claimed to be scholars yet possess no knowledge of the reality of this religion, have been corrupted by this deception!

It is well known that the servant, even if he believes in the Hereafter, by nature will require the necessities of this world, will require the promotion of good and the repression of harm. If such a person believes that following the True Religion, being firm upon *Tawḥīd* and the *Sunnah*, negates this natural instinct, that by following it he will be forced to undergo an unbearable amount of tribulation, and that he will lose out on any temporal benefit; for sure his desire to follow this religion will weaken. He will move from being amongst the ranks of the Forerunners to being amongst the ranks of those who take a medium course, perhaps even to being among the ranks of those who oppress themselves or the ranks of the hypocrites! The Prophet (ﷺ) said,

> Rush to doing good deeds [before you are overtaken] by tribulation which would be like a part of the dark night. A man would awake as a Muslim and go to sleep as a disbeliever and he would go to sleep as a Muslim and awake as a disbeliever; he would sell his faith for some worldly gain.[3]

This is because if he starts to believe that by following this religion, his worldly life will be ruined, he will face adversity and harm that he cannot bear, and lose out on any chance of attaining what he requires to live; he will never allow himself to be placed in such a situation. Glory be to Allāh, far removed is He from any imperfection! How many are the people who have been deceived by this false notion into not implementing this religion fully! This notion arises from being ignorant of the reality of this religion and being ignorant about the reality of bless-

[3] Muslim [#186] on the authority of Abū Hurayrah (*raḍiyAllāhu ʿanhu*)

ings and bliss, and gives birth to the person turning away from the reality of the religion and turning away from seeking true bliss.

It is well known that the servant only becomes happy and fulfilled when he actually knows the bliss which he desires, loves to attain that bliss, knows those actions that lead to it and has the firm resolve to enact those deeds. Knowing what one desires is not enough to attain that desire if unaccompanied with action, having a firm resolve to do something does not bring that thing into being if unaccompanied by *ṣabr.* Allāh, Exalted is He says,

وَٱلْعَصْرِ ۝١ إِنَّ ٱلْإِنسَٰنَ لَفِى خُسْرٍ ۝٢ إِلَّا ٱلَّذِينَ ءَامَنُوا۟ وَعَمِلُوا۟ ٱلصَّٰلِحَٰتِ وَتَوَاصَوْا۟ بِٱلْحَقِّ وَتَوَاصَوْا۟ بِٱلصَّبْرِ ۝٣

«By time, truly man is in loss - except for those who have faith do righteous deeds and urge each other to truth and urge each other to steadfastness»

[*al-'Aṣr* (103): 1-3]

The point of discussion here is that the two foundations that lead to this false notion are built upon ignorance of the Command of Allāh, His religion, His promise and His threat.

When a person comes to believe that he is completely fulfilling the obligations upon him and avoiding the prohibitions; inwardly and outwardly, such a person is ignorant of the True Religion, the great right that Allāh has over him and what is required of him. Therefore he is ignorant of the right of Allāh upon him and what he himself possesses of religiosity. If he believes that subjugation and oppression lies in store for the believers and victory for the disbelievers and hypocrites, he is also ignorant of the promise of Allāh and His threat.

With regards the first issue, often is a person lacking in knowledge because of which he leaves various obligations, moreover those obligations he does know of, many does he fall short of in completing or even leaves them. He leaves them either because of laziness, negligence, false interpretation, blind following, or the belief that he is doing something more important than that obligation. The obligations of the heart are greater and more important then the obligations of the body, yet many people leave them and deem them something merely recommended! You could see a person grieving at leaving a bodily obligation yet has no concern for the fact that he has left a greater obligation of the heart; he grieves at committing the least sin yet has no concern that his heart is committing far greater sins!

How many are the people who leave what Allāh has obligated upon them, believing that by doing so they are worshipping Allāh! They leave enjoining the good and prohibiting the evil, while having the ability to change the evil, presuming that by doing so they are leaving alone matters that do not concern them. Such people are from the worst of creation, even though they may think that they are fulfilling the rights of faith and are the *Awliyā*'!

How many are the people who worship Allāh through doing something that He has prohibited, thinking that they are drawing closer to Him. These people do things such as listening to music and poetry in song form and use this to draw closer to Allāh, thinking all the while that they are the *Awliyā*' of the All-Merciful!

How many are the people who think they are wrongly oppressed, that they themselves are not in the wrong at all when the reality is quite different. Rather they could be in the right in some matters and be in the wrong in others and hence themselves be oppressors in the latter. Ones love of something causes him to be blinded and deafened by it, man, by nature, loves himself and hates his enemy; hence he will always see his own good qualities and his enemies bad qualities. This state could go to such an extreme that a man could start believing his evil deeds to be good deeds,

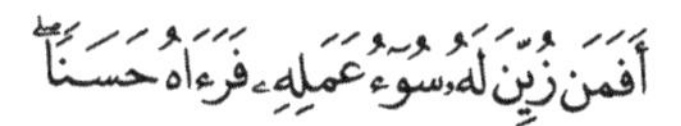

«And what of him the evil of whose actions appears fine to him so that he sees them as good?»
[*al-Fāṭir* (35): 8]

and the good deeds of his enemy as evil, as the poet said,

They looked with the eye of enmity, were they to have looked with the eye of pleasure
They would have regarded to be good what they had thought to be evil

Much of what the people take as religion are but habits and ways taken from their forefathers, blindly followed. Allāh, Glorious is He, has only guaranteed victory for His *Awliyā'* who adhere firmly to His religion by way of knowledge and action. He has not guaranteed victory for falsehood, even if the one following it believes it to be correct. Similarly, nobility, honour and supremacy lies in store for those who adhere firmly to the faith with which Allāh sent the Messengers and revealed the Books: in knowledge, action and belief,

وَأَنتُمُ ٱلْأَعْلَوْنَ إِن كُنتُم مُّؤْمِنِينَ

«You will be uppermost if your are believers»
[*Āli 'Imrān* (3): 139]

وَلِلَّهِ ٱلْعِزَّةُ وَلِرَسُولِهِۦ وَلِلْمُؤْمِنِينَ

«...but all might belongs to Allāh and to His Messenger and the believers»
[*al-Munāfiqūn* (63): 8]

So the servant is allotted supremacy, might and honour in accordance to his faith and his establishment of its realities. So if he is lacking in any aspect of this, it is because he is lacking in aspects of faith, either in knowledge or action, inwardly or outwardly. Likewise Allāh defends the believers in accordance to their faith,

«Allāh will defend those who have faith»
[*al-Ḥajj* (22): 38]

So if the defence is lacking in anyway, it is because of our own weakness in faith. Likewise, Allāh suffices us is in accordance to our faith,

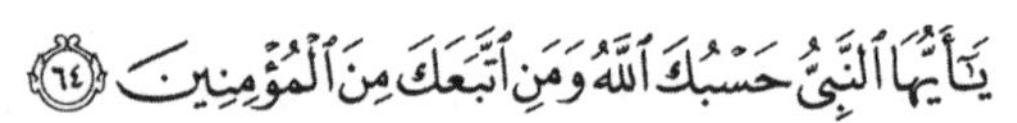

«O Prophet! Allāh is enough for you and for the believers who follow you»
[*al-Anfāl* (8): 64]

So as faith increases and decreases, Allāh's sufficing for us also increases and decreases, it is the belief of *Ahlu-Sunnah wa-l-Jamā'ah* that faith increases and decreases.

The same applies to the *wilāyah* of Allāh,

وَٱللَّهُ وَلِيُّ ٱلْمُؤْمِنِينَ ﴿٦٨﴾

«Allāh is the Protector of the believers»

[*Āli 'Imrān* (3): 68]

ٱللَّهُ وَلِيُّ ٱلَّذِينَ ءَامَنُوا۟

«Allāh is the Protector of those who have faith»

[*al-Baqarah* (2): 257]

The same applies to Allāh being with us in the specific sense reserved for the believers,

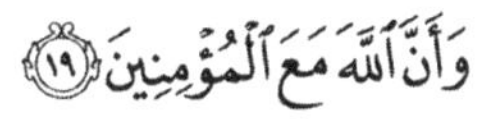

«Allāh is with the believers»

[*al-Anfāl* (8): 19]

The same applies to total support and victory,

إِنَّا لَنَنصُرُ رُسُلَنَا وَٱلَّذِينَ ءَامَنُوا۟ فِى ٱلْحَيَوٰةِ ٱلدُّنْيَا
وَيَوْمَ يَقُومُ ٱلْأَشْهَـٰدُ ﴿٥١﴾

«We will certainly help Our Messengers and those who have faith both in the life of this world and on the Day the witnesses appear»

[*al-Ghāfir* (40): 51]

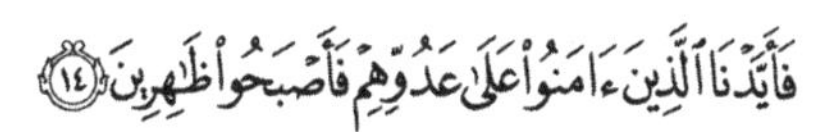

«So We supported those who had faith against their enemy and they became victorious»

[*as-Saff* (61): 14]

This is why, if the servant is tried, either in body, wealth or being defeated by his enemy, the only reason for this is his sins - either his leaving something obligatory or his committing something prohibited which is part and parcel of his diminishing in faith. Through understanding this well do we remove any potential difficulty in understanding His saying,

وَلَن يَجْعَلَ ٱللَّهُ لِلْكَٰفِرِينَ عَلَى ٱلْمُؤْمِنِينَ سَبِيلًا ﴿١٤١﴾

«Allāh will not give the disbelievers any way against the believers»

[*an-Nisā'* (4): 141]

Some people understand this verse to refer to the Hereafter and others understand it to be a reference to proof and clarity of truth. The correct position is that it is to be understood in the same light as the previously quoted verses; the true and complete believer will never be overcome by the believers, but if there is a weakness in faith, the disbelievers will find ways against them in accordance to that lack of faith.

The believer is noble, victorious, aided, sufficed and defended wherever he may be, even if the whole of mankind were to gather against him, provided that he has fulfilled the reality of faith both in speech and deed. Allāh, Exalted is He, has said to the believers,

وَلَا تَهِنُوا۟ وَلَا تَحْزَنُوا۟ وَأَنتُمُ ٱلْأَعْلَوْنَ إِن كُنتُم مُّؤْمِنِينَ

«Do not give up and do not be downhearted. You will be uppermost if you are believers»

[*Āli 'Imrān* (3): 139]

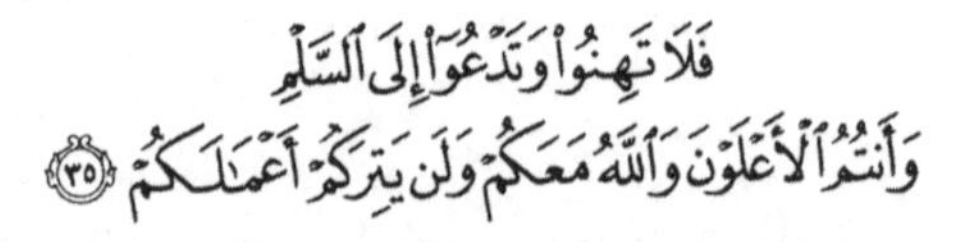

«Do not become faint hearted and call for peace when you are uppermost and Allāh is with you - He would never cheat you of your deeds»

[*Muhammad* (47): 35]

This guarantee is conditional upon their faith and deeds, deeds which are in reality an army from the armies of Allāh.

With regards the second issue, the issue of promise and threat, many people think that the lot of the believers in this world is humiliation and subjugation and as such they do not fully believe in Allāh's promise to aid His religion and His servants. Such a person believes that such promises are tied to a particular group of people or a particular time, an understanding arising from lack of trust in the promise of Allāh and poor comprehension of His Book.

Allāh, Glorious is He, has made clear in His Book that He will aid the believers in this world and the next,

إِنَّا لَنَنصُرُ رُسُلَنَا وَٱلَّذِينَ ءَامَنُوا۟ فِى ٱلْحَيَوٰةِ ٱلدُّنْيَا
وَيَوْمَ يَقُومُ ٱلْأَشْهَـٰدُ ﴿٥١﴾

«We will certainly help Our Messengers and those who have faith both in the life of this world and on the Day the witnesses appear»

[*al-Ghāfir* (40): 51]

وَمَن يَتَوَلَّ ٱللَّهَ
وَرَسُولَهُۥ وَٱلَّذِينَ ءَامَنُوا۟ فَإِنَّ حِزْبَ ٱللَّهِ هُمُ ٱلْغَـٰلِبُونَ ﴿٥٦﴾

«As for those who make Allāh their friend, and His Messenger and those who have faith: it is the party of Allāh who are victorious»

[*al-Mā'idah* (5): 55]

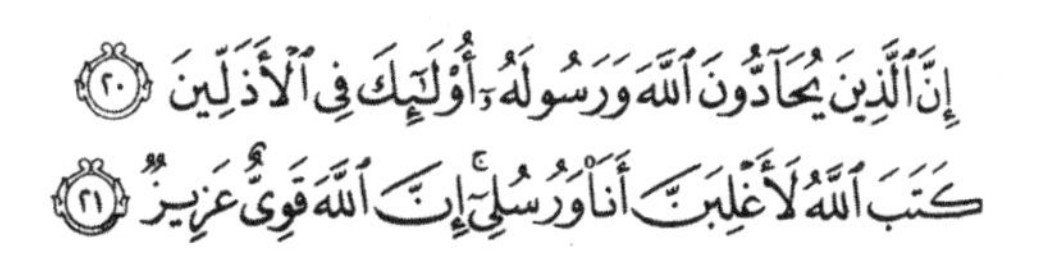

> **«Those who oppose Allāh and His Messenger, such people will be among the most abased. Allāh has decreed, 'I will be victorious, I and My Messengers'»**
>
> [*al-Mujādilah* (58): 20-21]

There are many such verses in the Qur'ān. Allāh, Glorious is He, has explained that what the servant is afflicted with of trial or subjugation or the likes is because of his sins, as such any difficulty in understanding these verses is completely removed and their no longer remains any need for far fetched interpretations.

Returning back to the first issue, Allāh has explained this in a number of different ways, some of which have been previously mentioned. Allāh also censures those who look to other than the believers for support and nobility,

﴿ يَا أَيُّهَا الَّذِينَ آمَنُوا لَا تَتَّخِذُوا الْيَهُودَ وَالنَّصَارَىٰ أَوْلِيَاءَ بَعْضُهُمْ
أَوْلِيَاءُ بَعْضٍ وَمَن يَتَوَلَّهُم مِّنكُمْ فَإِنَّهُ مِنْهُمْ إِنَّ اللَّهَ لَا يَهْدِي الْقَوْمَ
الظَّالِمِينَ ﴿٥١﴾ فَتَرَى الَّذِينَ فِي قُلُوبِهِم مَّرَضٌ يُسَارِعُونَ فِيهِمْ
يَقُولُونَ نَخْشَىٰ أَن تُصِيبَنَا دَائِرَةٌ فَعَسَى اللَّهُ أَن يَأْتِيَ بِالْفَتْحِ أَوْ أَمْرٍ
مِّنْ عِندِهِ فَيُصْبِحُوا عَلَىٰ مَا أَسَرُّوا فِي أَنفُسِهِمْ نَادِمِينَ ﴿٥٢﴾
وَيَقُولُ الَّذِينَ آمَنُوا أَهَٰؤُلَاءِ الَّذِينَ أَقْسَمُوا بِاللَّهِ جَهْدَ أَيْمَانِهِمْ
إِنَّهُمْ لَمَعَكُمْ حَبِطَتْ أَعْمَالُهُمْ فَأَصْبَحُوا خَاسِرِينَ ﴿٥٣﴾ يَا أَيُّهَا
الَّذِينَ آمَنُوا مَن يَرْتَدَّ مِنكُمْ عَن دِينِهِ فَسَوْفَ يَأْتِي اللَّهُ بِقَوْمٍ يُحِبُّهُمْ
وَيُحِبُّونَهُ أَذِلَّةٍ عَلَى الْمُؤْمِنِينَ أَعِزَّةٍ عَلَى الْكَافِرِينَ يُجَاهِدُونَ فِي
سَبِيلِ اللَّهِ وَلَا يَخَافُونَ لَوْمَةَ لَائِمٍ ذَٰلِكَ فَضْلُ اللَّهِ يُؤْتِيهِ مَن يَشَاءُ
وَاللَّهُ وَاسِعٌ عَلِيمٌ ﴿٥٤﴾ إِنَّمَا وَلِيُّكُمُ اللَّهُ وَرَسُولُهُ وَالَّذِينَ آمَنُوا الَّذِينَ

يُقِيمُونَ ٱلصَّلَوٰةَ وَيُؤْتُونَ ٱلزَّكَوٰةَ وَهُمْ رَٰكِعُونَ ﴿٥٥﴾ وَمَن يَتَوَلَّ ٱللَّهَ
وَرَسُولَهُۥ وَٱلَّذِينَ ءَامَنُوا۟ فَإِنَّ حِزْبَ ٱللَّهِ هُمُ ٱلْغَٰلِبُونَ ﴿٥٦﴾

«You who have faith! Do not take the Jews and Christians as your friends; they are friends of one another. Any of you who takes them as friends is one of them. Allāh does not guide wrongdoing people. Yet you see those with sickness in their hearts rushing to them, saying, 'we fear the wheel of fate may turn against us.' But it may well be that Allāh will bring about victory or some other contingency from Him. Then they will deeply regret their secret thoughts. Those who have faith say, 'are these the people who swore by Allāh, with their most earnest oaths, that they were with you?' Their actions have come to nothing and they now are the losers. You who have faith! If any of you renounce your religion, Allāh will bring forward a people whom He loves and who love Him, humble to the believers, fierce against the disbelievers, who do Jihād in the way of Allāh and do not fear the blame of the censurer. That is the unbounded favour of Allāh which He gives to whoever He wills. Allāh is Boundless, All-Knowing. Your friend is only Allāh and His Messenger and those who have faith: those who establish the prayer and give the zakāt and bow. As for those who make Allāh their friend, and His Messenger and those who have faith: it is the party of Allāh who are victorious»

[*al-Mā'idah* (5): 51-56]

بَشِّرِ ٱلْمُنَٰفِقِينَ بِأَنَّ لَهُمْ عَذَابًا أَلِيمًا ﴿١٣٨﴾ ٱلَّذِينَ يَتَّخِذُونَ ٱلْكَٰفِرِينَ أَوْلِيَآءَ مِن دُونِ ٱلْمُؤْمِنِينَ ۚ أَيَبْتَغُونَ عِندَهُمُ ٱلْعِزَّةَ فَإِنَّ ٱلْعِزَّةَ لِلَّهِ جَمِيعًا ﴿١٣٩﴾

«Give glad tidings to the hypocrites that they will have a painful punishment, those who take the disbelievers as friends and protectors rather than the believers. Do they hope to find power and strength with them? Power and strength belongs entirely to Allāh»

[*an-Nisā'* (4): 138-139]

﴿٧﴾ يَقُولُونَ لَئِن رَّجَعْنَآ إِلَى ٱلْمَدِينَةِ لَيُخْرِجَنَّ ٱلْأَعَزُّ مِنْهَا ٱلْأَذَلَّ ۚ وَلِلَّهِ ٱلْعِزَّةُ وَلِرَسُولِهِۦ وَلِلْمُؤْمِنِينَ وَلَٰكِنَّ ٱلْمُنَٰفِقِينَ لَا يَعْلَمُونَ ﴿٨﴾

«They say, 'if we return to Madīnah, the mightier will drive out the inferior.' But all might belongs to Allāh and His Messenger and the believers. But the hypocrites do not know this»

[*al-Munāfiqūn* (63): 8]

مَن كَانَ يُرِيدُ ٱلْعِزَّةَ فَلِلَّهِ ٱلْعِزَّةُ جَمِيعًا ۚ إِلَيْهِ يَصْعَدُ ٱلْكَلِمُ ٱلطَّيِّبُ وَٱلْعَمَلُ ٱلصَّٰلِحُ يَرْفَعُهُۥ ۚ

«If anyone wants power, all power belongs to Allāh. All good words rise to Him and virtuous deeds raises it»

[*Fāṭir* (35): 10]

Meaning that whoever wants power, let him seek it through obeying Allāh. Allāh, Exalted is He, also says,

هُوَ ٱلَّذِىٓ أَرۡسَلَ رَسُولَهُۥ بِٱلۡهُدَىٰ وَدِينِ
ٱلۡحَقِّ لِيُظۡهِرَهُۥ عَلَى ٱلدِّينِ كُلِّهِۦۚ وَكَفَىٰ بِٱللَّهِ شَهِيدٗا ﴿٢٨﴾

«It is He who sent His Messenger with the guidance and the religion of truth to exalt it over every other religion...»

[*al-Fatḥ* (48): 28]

يَٰٓأَيُّهَا ٱلَّذِينَ ءَامَنُواْ هَلۡ أَدُلُّكُمۡ
عَلَىٰ تِجَٰرَةٖ تُنجِيكُم مِّنۡ عَذَابٍ أَلِيمٖ ﴿١٠﴾ تُؤۡمِنُونَ بِٱللَّهِ وَرَسُولِهِۦ وَتُجَٰهِدُونَ
فِي سَبِيلِ ٱللَّهِ بِأَمۡوَٰلِكُمۡ وَأَنفُسِكُمۡۚ ذَٰلِكُمۡ خَيۡرٞ لَّكُمۡ إِن كُنتُمۡ تَعۡلَمُونَ ﴿١١﴾
يَغۡفِرۡ لَكُمۡ ذُنُوبَكُمۡ وَيُدۡخِلۡكُمۡ جَنَّٰتٖ تَجۡرِي مِن تَحۡتِهَا ٱلۡأَنۡهَٰرُ وَمَسَٰكِنَ
طَيِّبَةٗ فِي جَنَّٰتِ عَدۡنٖۚ ذَٰلِكَ ٱلۡفَوۡزُ ٱلۡعَظِيمُ ﴿١٢﴾ وَأُخۡرَىٰ تُحِبُّونَهَاۖ نَصۡرٞ
مِّنَ ٱللَّهِ وَفَتۡحٞ قَرِيبٞۗ وَبَشِّرِ ٱلۡمُؤۡمِنِينَ ﴿١٣﴾ يَٰٓأَيُّهَا ٱلَّذِينَ ءَامَنُواْ كُونُوٓاْ
أَنصَارَ ٱللَّهِ كَمَا قَالَ عِيسَى ٱبۡنُ مَرۡيَمَ لِلۡحَوَارِيِّـۧنَ مَنۡ أَنصَارِيٓ إِلَى ٱللَّهِۖ
قَالَ ٱلۡحَوَارِيُّونَ نَحۡنُ أَنصَارُ ٱللَّهِۖ فَـَٔامَنَت طَّآئِفَةٞ مِّنۢ بَنِيٓ إِسۡرَٰٓءِيلَ
وَكَفَرَت طَّآئِفَةٞۖ فَأَيَّدۡنَا ٱلَّذِينَ ءَامَنُواْ عَلَىٰ عَدُوِّهِمۡ فَأَصۡبَحُواْ ظَٰهِرِينَ ﴿١٤﴾

«You have faith! Shall I direct you to a transaction which will save you from a painful punishment? It is to have faith in Allāh and His Messenger and do Jihād in the Way of Allāh with your wealth and your selves. That is better for you if you only knew. He will forgive you your wrong actions and admit you into Gardens with rivers flowing under them, and fine dwellings in the Gardens of Eden. That is the great victory. And other things you love: support from Allāh and imminent victory. Give good news to

the believers! You who have faith! Be helpers of Allāh as 'Īsā son of Maryam said to the Disciples, 'who will be my helpers to Allāh?' The Disciples said, 'we will be the helpers of Allāh.' One faction of the tribe had faith and the others were disbelievers. So We supported those who had faith against their enemy and they became victorious»

[*as-Ṣaff* (61): 10-14]

Allāh, Exalted is He, said to 'Īsā,

إِذْ قَالَ ٱللَّهُ يَٰعِيسَىٰٓ إِنِّى مُتَوَفِّيكَ وَرَافِعُكَ
إِلَىَّ وَمُطَهِّرُكَ مِنَ ٱلَّذِينَ كَفَرُوا۟ وَجَاعِلُ ٱلَّذِينَ ٱتَّبَعُوكَ
فَوْقَ ٱلَّذِينَ كَفَرُوٓا۟ إِلَىٰ يَوْمِ ٱلْقِيَٰمَةِ

«...I will take you back and raise you up to Me and purify you of those who disbelieve. And I will place the people who follow you above the disbelievers until the Day of Rising»

[*Āli 'Imrān* (3): 55]

Because the Christians followed him in some fashion, Allāh placed them above the Jews until the Day of Rising. Because the Muslims truly follow him, Allāh placed them above the Christians until the Day of Rising. Allāh, Exalted is He, says to the believers,

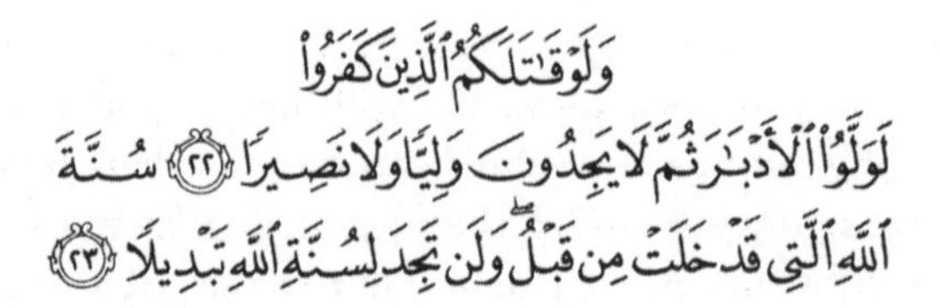

«If those who disbelieve should fight you, they would turn their backs and then find no one to

protect or help them. That is Allāh's pattern which has passed away before. You will not find any change in the pattern of Allāh»

[*al-Fatḥ* (48): 22-23]

This address is directed to the believers who have fully established the rights of faith, outwardly and inwardly. Allāh, Exalted is He, says,

وَٱلْعَٰقِبَةُ لِلْمُتَّقِينَ

«The successful outcome is for those who have taqwā»

[*al-A'rāf* (7): 128]

وَٱلْعَٰقِبَةُ لِلتَّقْوَىٰ

«The best end result is gained by taqwā»

[*Ṭā Hā* (20): 132]

meaning: the end result in this world before the Hereafter. This is because this was mentioned after having mentioned the story of Nūḥ and his *ṣabr* and being aided against his people. Then Allāh, Exalted is He, says,

«That is some of the news of the unseen which We reveal to you. Neither you nor your people knew it before this time. So be steadfast. The best result is for those who have taqwā»

[*Hūd* (11): 49]

meaning: the result of aid and victory is for you and those

with you just as it was for Nūḥ and those with him.

Similarly, Allāh says,

وَأْمُرْ أَهْلَكَ بِٱلصَّلَوٰةِ
وَٱصْطَبِرْ عَلَيْهَا ۖ لَا نَسْـَٔلُكَ رِزْقًا ۖ نَّحْنُ نَرْزُقُكَ ۗ وَٱلْعَـٰقِبَةُ لِلتَّقْوَىٰ

«Instruct your family to perform the prayer and be constant in it. We do not ask you for provision, We provide for you. And the best end result is gained by taqwā»

[*Ṭā Ḥā* (20): 132]

وَإِن تَصْبِرُوا۟ وَتَتَّقُوا۟ لَا يَضُرُّكُمْ كَيْدُهُمْ شَيْـًٔا ۗ

«But if you are steadfast and have taqwā, their scheming will not harm you in any way»

[*Āli 'Imrān* (3): 120]

بَلَىٰٓ ۚ إِن تَصْبِرُوا۟ وَتَتَّقُوا۟ وَيَأْتُوكُم مِّن فَوْرِهِمْ
هَـٰذَا يُمْدِدْكُمْ رَبُّكُم بِخَمْسَةِ ءَالَـٰفٍ مِّنَ ٱلْمَلَـٰٓئِكَةِ مُسَوِّمِينَ

«Yes indeed! But if you are steadfast and have taqwā and they come upon you suddenly, your Lord will reinforce you with five thousand Angels, clearly identified»

[*Āli 'Imrān* (3): 125]

قَالَ أَنَا۠ يُوسُفُ وَهَـٰذَآ أَخِى ۖ قَدْ مَنَّ ٱللَّهُ
عَلَيْنَآ ۖ إِنَّهُۥ مَن يَتَّقِ وَيَصْبِرْ فَإِنَّ ٱللَّهَ لَا يُضِيعُ أَجْرَ
ٱلْمُحْسِنِينَ ﴿٩٠﴾

«...I am Yūsuf and here is my brother. Allāh has acted graciously to us, As for those who have

taqwā and are steadfast, Allāh does not allow to go to waste the wage of those who do good»

[*Yūsuf* (12): 90]

يَٰٓأَيُّهَا ٱلَّذِينَ ءَامَنُوٓا۟ إِن تَتَّقُوا۟
ٱللَّهَ يَجْعَل لَّكُمْ فُرْقَانًا وَيُكَفِّرْ عَنكُمْ سَيِّـَٔاتِكُمْ وَيَغْفِرْ
لَكُمْ وَٱللَّهُ ذُو ٱلْفَضْلِ ٱلْعَظِيمِ ﴿٢٩﴾

«You who have faith! If you have taqwā of Allāh, He will give you discrimination and erase your bad deeds from you and forgive you...»

[*al-Anfāl* (8): 29]

meaning by discrimination here nobility, aid, victory and light that distinguishes truth from falsehood.

مَن يَتَّقِ ٱللَّهَ يَجْعَل لَّهُۥ مَخْرَجًا ﴿٢﴾ وَيَرْزُقْهُ
مِنْ حَيْثُ لَا يَحْتَسِبُ وَمَن يَتَوَكَّلْ عَلَى ٱللَّهِ فَهُوَ حَسْبُهُۥٓ إِنَّ ٱللَّهَ
بَٰلِغُ أَمْرِهِۦ قَدْ جَعَلَ ٱللَّهُ لِكُلِّ شَىْءٍ قَدْرًا ﴿٣﴾

«Whoever has taqwā of Allāh - He will give him a way out and provide for him from where he does not expect. Whoever puts his trust in Allāh - He will be enough for him. Allāh always achieves His aim, Allāh has appointed a measure for all things»

[*at-Ṭalāq* (65): 2-3]

Ibn Mājah and ibn Abī ad-Dunyā record on the authority of Abū Dharr (*raḍiyAllāhu ʿanhu*) that the Prophet (ﷺ) said,

Were the people to act by this verse, it would suffice

them[4]

Now returning back to the second issue, Allāh Exalted is He says,

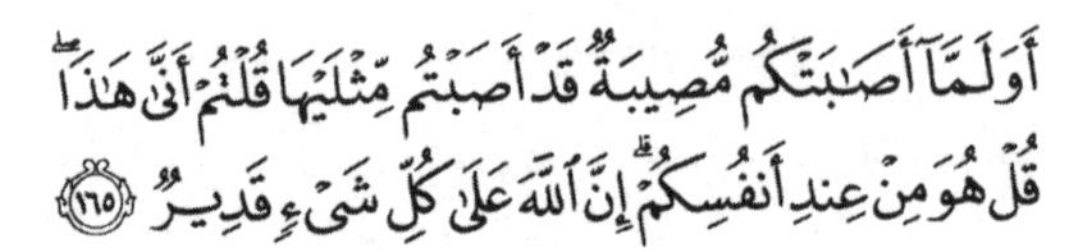

«Why is it when calamity happens to you, when you have already afflicted twice as much, you say, 'how could this possibly happen?' Say, 'it has come from your own selves'...»

[*Āli 'Imrān* (3): 165]

إِنَّ ٱلَّذِينَ تَوَلَّوْا۟ مِنكُمْ
يَوْمَ ٱلْتَقَى ٱلْجَمْعَانِ إِنَّمَا ٱسْتَزَلَّهُمُ ٱلشَّيْطَٰنُ بِبَعْضِ مَا
كَسَبُوا۟ وَلَقَدْ عَفَا ٱللَّهُ عَنْهُمْ ۗ إِنَّ ٱللَّهَ غَفُورٌ حَلِيمٌ ﴿١٥٥﴾

«Those of you who turned their backs on the day the two armies clashed - it was Satan who made them slip for what they had done...»

[*Āli 'Imrān* (3): 155]

وَمَآ أَصَٰبَكُم مِّن مُّصِيبَةٍ فَبِمَا
كَسَبَتْ أَيْدِيكُمْ وَيَعْفُوا۟ عَن كَثِيرٍ ﴿٣٠﴾

«Any disaster that strikes you is through what your own hands have earned and He pardons much»

[*ash-Shūrā* (42): 30]

---

[4] Aḥmad [#21551] and ibn Mājah [#4220]. It was declared ṣaḥīḥ by ibn Ḥibbān [#6669] and al-Ḥākim [#3819] with adh-Dhahabī agreeing.

ظَهَرَ ٱلْفَسَادُ فِى ٱلْبَرِّ وَٱلْبَحْرِ بِمَا كَسَبَتْ
أَيْدِى ٱلنَّاسِ لِيُذِيقَهُم بَعْضَ ٱلَّذِى عَمِلُوا۟ لَعَلَّهُمْ يَرْجِعُونَ ﴿٤١﴾

«Corruption has appeared in both land and sea because of what people's own hands have brought about so that they may taste something of what they have done so that hopefully they will turn back»

[*ar-Rūm* (30): 41]

وَإِنَّآ إِذَآ
أَذَقْنَا ٱلْإِنسَٰنَ مِنَّا رَحْمَةً فَرِحَ بِهَا ۖ وَإِن تُصِبْهُمْ سَيِّئَةٌۢ
بِمَا قَدَّمَتْ أَيْدِيهِمْ فَإِنَّ ٱلْإِنسَٰنَ كَفُورٌ ﴿٤٨﴾

«When We let man taste mercy from Us he exults in it. But if something bad strikes him for what he has done, he is ungrateful»

[*ash-Shūrā* (42): 48]

وَإِذَآ أَذَقْنَا
ٱلنَّاسَ رَحْمَةً فَرِحُوا۟ بِهَا ۖ وَإِن تُصِبْهُمْ سَيِّئَةٌۢ بِمَا قَدَّمَتْ أَيْدِيهِمْ
إِذَا هُمْ يَقْنَطُونَ ﴿٣٦﴾

«When We give people a taste of mercy, they rejoice in it, but when something bad happens to them because of what they themselves have done, they immediately lose all hope»

[*ar-Rūm* (30): 36]

أَوْ يُوبِقْهُنَّ بِمَا كَسَبُوا۟ وَيَعْفُ عَن كَثِيرٍ ﴿٣٤﴾

«...or He wrecks them for what they have earned

though He pardons much»

[*ash-Shūrā* (42): 34]

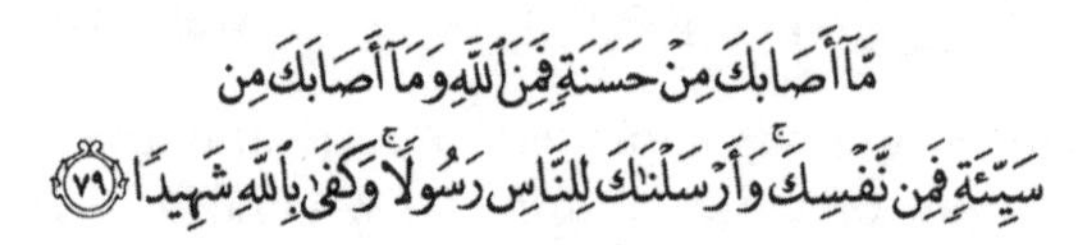

«Any good thing that happens to you is from Allāh. Any bad thing that happens to you comes from yourself...»

[*an-Nisā'* (4): 79]

This is why Allāh, Glorious is He, ordered His Messenger and the believers with following what is revealed to them, which is to obey Him and to await His promise. He ordered them to ask forgiveness and to have *ṣabr* for the servant will always fall into some type of deficiency or extremism. Therefore he must await the promise with *ṣabr* and perfect his worship through asking forgiveness. Moreover through *ṣabr* does a person increase in certainty about the promise. Allāh, Exalted is He, has mentioned both of these in His saying,

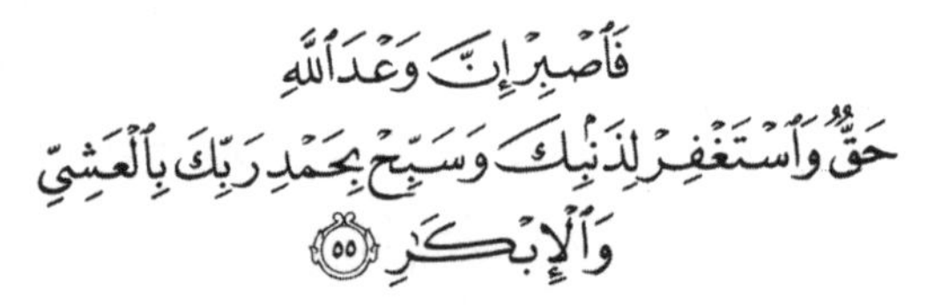

«So remain steadfast. Allāh's promise is true. Ask forgiveness for your wrong action and glorify your Lord with praise in the evening and the early morning»

[*al-Ghāfir* (40): 55]

Allāh, Glorious is He, has mentioned the stories of His Prophets and their followers and how they were victorious through *ṣabr* and obedience in His Book,

لَقَدْ كَانَ فِي قَصَصِهِمْ عِبْرَةٌ لِّأُولِي ٱلْأَلْبَٰبِ

«There is instruction in their stories for people of intelligence»

[*Yūsuf* (12): 111]

To complete this point, a number of principles need to be understood.

1. What the Muslims are afflicted with of evil, trials, tribulations and harm is less than that which the disbelievers are afflicted with and practical experience testifies to the truth of this fact. In a similar fashion the righteous are afflicted less in this world than the sinners, the transgressors and the oppressors.

2. When the believers are afflicted with something, they place themselves in the state of *riḍā* and *iḥtisāb*[5], if they are unable to achieve *riḍā* they recourse to *ṣabr* and *iḥtisāb*, this in turn lightens the burden of the tribulation. Each time they see the return of their efforts it becomes easier to bear the difficulty. The disbelievers are not able to recourse to *riḍā* or have *iḥtisāb*, and if they show *ṣabr*, it is the *ṣabr* of animals. Allāh, Exalted is He, informs us of this with His words,

وَلَا تَهِنُوا۟ فِي ٱبْتِغَآءِ ٱلْقَوْمِ ۖ إِن تَكُونُوا۟ تَأْلَمُونَ فَإِنَّهُمْ يَأْلَمُونَ كَمَا تَأْلَمُونَ ۖ وَتَرْجُونَ مِنَ ٱللَّهِ مَا لَا يَرْجُونَ

[5] *Iḥtisāb*: being expectant of reward from Allāh. al-Kafawī, *al-Kulliyyāt* [p. 57] said, '*Iḥtisāb* is to seek reward from Allāh through showing *ṣabr* at times of tribulation and adversity, with the soul at peace not disliking what it has been afflicted with.'

> **«Do not relax in pursuit of the enemy. If you feel pain, they too are feeling it just as you are, but you hope for something from Allāh which they cannot hope for»**
>
> [*an-Nisā'* (4): 104]

Hence both groups felt pain, but the believers are distinguished by hoping for reward and drawing close to Allāh, Exalted is He.

3. When the believers are afflicted, they are afflicted in accordance to their level of faith, actions of obedience and sincerity. The believer is able to bear such affliction that would have been unbearable by any other. This is part and parcel of Allāh's defending the believers, for Allāh holds back much trial and tribulation from His servants, and that trial that does come their way, is something that is within their ability to bear, and has been lightened further.

4. The more love becomes firmly embedded in the heart, easier does it become for the lover to endure harm and adversity in the pursuit of pleasing his beloved. Indeed true lovers boast about such occasions in the presence of their beloved, as one of them said,

Were you to choose to afflict me with adversity
Truly delighted would I be that I crossed your mind

So what then would one think of loving the Greatest object of love, Whose trial of His beloved is pure mercy and beneficence?

5. What is seen of the disbeliever, the sinner and the hypocrite gaining ascendancy, might and position, is far less than what is gained by the believer. Indeed the reality of what is gained by the first is disgrace, subjugation and ignominy, even though the outward appearance of things may seem different. al-Ḥasan, may Allāh have mercy upon him, said, 'they, even though they have masses of horses and mules subservient to them, the ignominy of sin is in their hearts and Allāh will only ever disgrace those who disobey Him.'

6. The believer facing tribulation is like medicine, it removes such disease from him that were it to have endured, it would have destroyed him, or at the very least diminished his reward and ranking. Trials and tribulations extract that disease and prepare him to receive complete reward and lofty ranking. With this is mind, it is understood that the existence of this, with respect to the believer, is better for him than its absence. The Prophet (ﷺ) said,

> By the One in Whose hands is my soul, there is no decree that Allāh determines for the believer except that it is good for him, and this only applies to the believer. If he meets with times of ease and plentitude, he thanks Allāh and that is good for him. If he meets with times of adversity, he is patient and that is good for him.

Therefore trial and tribulation is from the means of Allāh aiding His servant, ennobling him and granting him well-being. It is for this reason that the most severely tried people were the Prophets, then those closest to them, each person being tried in accordance to his religion. The believer is afflicted with tribulation to such an extent that he ends up walking on the earth with no trace of sin remaining on him.

7. What the believer is afflicted of in this world, matters such as being defeated and overcome by his enemy, or being harmed by him, is something that is necessary and unavoidable, just like extreme heat and cold, illnesses, worries and distress. These matters are part and parcel of living in this world and having the nature that man does. Even children and animals face this as determined by the wisdom of the All-Wise. Were evil to be completely separated from good, benefit from harm, and delight from pain; this would be a totally different world lacking the all encompassing wisdom that has mingled these matters, one with the other. These matters, existing entirely on their own, are only to be found in another Abode,

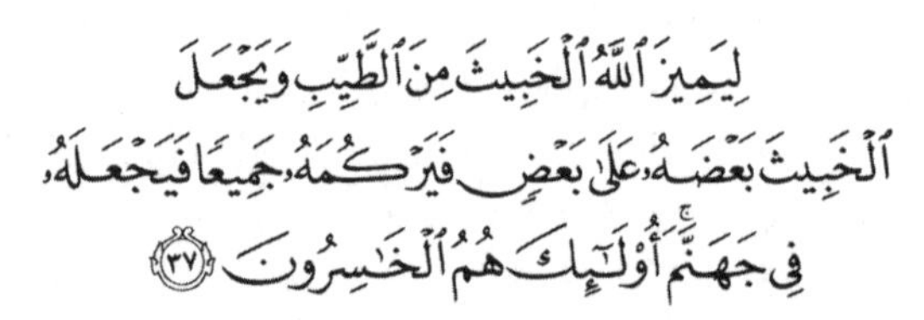

«...so that Allāh can sift the bad out from the good, and pile the bad on top of one another, heaping them all together, and tip them into Hell. They are the lost»

[*al-Anfāl* (8): 37]

8. In the believers being overcome and defeated by their enemy, in their being subjugated by them, lies great and profound wisdom which none knows in detail save Allāh, Mighty and Magnificent.

Amongst which is: their returning to the servitude of Allāh, humbling themselves before Him, realising their dire need of Him, and their sincerely asking Him to aid them in vanquishing their enemy. Were the Muslims always victorious, ever the leaders, they surely would have become vainglorious and insolent. Were the Muslims always defeated and subjugated, never would this religion have been established and never would their be a land ruled by the truth. Therefore the All-Wise determined that the Muslims be victorious sometimes and defeated other times. When they are defeated they turn back in humility to their Lord, submitting to Him and asking Him for forgiveness; when they are victorious, they establish His religion, enjoin the good and forbid the evil - striving against His enemies and coming to aid of His Awliyā'.

Amongst which is: were the Muslims always victorious, people would have accepted this religion for ulterior motives, motives other than religion and following the Messenger (ﷺ); and were the Muslims always defeated and subjugated, none would have accepted this religion. Therefore the All-Wise determined that the Muslims have sovereignty sometimes and at others times not and therefore sift those who intend Allāh and His Messenger from those who do not.

Amongst which is: Allāh loves that His servant show Him complete servitude in times of ease and difficulty, in times of well-being and tribulation, in times when they are in power and in times when they are subjugated. To Allāh belongs a servitude as dictated by the circumstances one finds himself in, it is these changing circumstances that serve to perfect servitude and make the heart firm. In the same way the body only becomes firm through experiencing heat and cold, hunger and thirst, weariness and labour, and their opposite. Therefore these trials and tribulations are actually a pre-requisite for the servants achieving perfection and achieving the firmness and uprightness that is sought of him.

Amongst which is: through the tribulation of being subjugated by their enemy, the Muslims are purified and refined. Allāh, Exalted is He, says concerning the wisdom behind the Muslim's defeat at the Battle of Uḥud,

وَلَا تَهِنُوا وَلَا تَحْزَنُوا وَأَنتُمُ الْأَعْلَوْنَ إِن كُنتُم مُّؤْمِنِينَ
﴿١٣٩﴾ إِن يَمْسَسْكُمْ قَرْحٌ فَقَدْ مَسَّ الْقَوْمَ قَرْحٌ مِّثْلُهُ ۚ
وَتِلْكَ الْأَيَّامُ نُدَاوِلُهَا بَيْنَ النَّاسِ وَلِيَعْلَمَ اللَّهُ الَّذِينَ
آمَنُوا وَيَتَّخِذَ مِنكُمْ شُهَدَاءَ ۗ وَاللَّهُ لَا يُحِبُّ الظَّالِمِينَ ﴿١٤٠﴾
وَلِيُمَحِّصَ اللَّهُ الَّذِينَ آمَنُوا وَيَمْحَقَ الْكَافِرِينَ ﴿١٤١﴾ أَمْ
حَسِبْتُمْ أَن تَدْخُلُوا الْجَنَّةَ وَلَمَّا يَعْلَمِ اللَّهُ الَّذِينَ جَاهَدُوا
مِنكُمْ وَيَعْلَمَ الصَّابِرِينَ ﴿١٤٢﴾ وَلَقَدْ كُنتُمْ تَمَنَّوْنَ الْمَوْتَ مِن
قَبْلِ أَن تَلْقَوْهُ فَقَدْ رَأَيْتُمُوهُ وَأَنتُمْ تَنظُرُونَ ﴿١٤٣﴾ وَمَا مُحَمَّدٌ
إِلَّا رَسُولٌ قَدْ خَلَتْ مِن قَبْلِهِ الرُّسُلُ ۚ أَفَإِن مَّاتَ أَوْ قُتِلَ
انقَلَبْتُمْ عَلَىٰ أَعْقَابِكُمْ ۚ وَمَن يَنقَلِبْ عَلَىٰ عَقِبَيْهِ فَلَن يَضُرَّ
اللَّهَ شَيْئًا ۗ وَسَيَجْزِي اللَّهُ الشَّاكِرِينَ ﴿١٤٤﴾

«Do not give up and do not be downhearted. You will be uppermost if you are believers. If you received a wound, they have already received a similar wound. We deal out such days to people turn by turn, so that Allāh will know those who have faith and can gather martyrs from among you - Allāh does not love the wrongdoers - and so that Allāh can purge those who have faith and wipe out the disbelievers. Or did you imagine that you were going to enter the Garden without Allāh knowing those among you who had struggled and knowing the steadfast? Muḥammad is only a Messenger and he has been preceded by other Messengers. If he were to die or be killed, would you turn on your heels?

Those who turn on their heels do not harm Allāh in any way. Allāh will recompense the thankful»
[*Āli 'Imrān* (3): 139-144]

In these verses, Allāh, Exalted is He, has mentioned numerous points of wisdom behind their defeat, after having assured them of being uppermost by virtue of their faith. He comforted them by saying that even though they had received a wound in obedience to Allāh and His Messenger, the disbelievers too had received a wound in disobedience to Allāh and His Messenger. Then He informed them that He deals out such days to people, turn by turn. Then He informed them that He did this so that He could know the believers; Allāh, Glorious is He, knows everything, before its existence and after its existence, but He desired to witness them in reality, and know their faith being lived out. Then He informed them that He desired to gather martyrs from among them; martyrdom holds an exalted ranking with Him, this exalted ranking can only be attained by being killed in His path, it is one of the most beloved things to Him and one of the most beneficial things for the servant. Then He informed them that He desired to purge and refine the believers; purge them of sin through their returning to Him in repentance, sins that were the cause of their defeat; and He also informed them that despite this, He wished to wipe out the disbelievers. Then He rejected their supposition that they would enter Paradise without *jihād* and *ṣabr*, were they always victorious, none would have fought them so that they could have undertaken *Jihād* and neither would they have had to display *ṣabr* at the harm inflicted them by their enemy.

These then are some of the points of wisdom behind the Muslims being defeated on occasion.

9. Allāh, Glorious is He, created the heavens and the earth and created life and death. He adorned the earth with what it contains in order to try His servants and examine them so that He could know those who desire what lies with Him as opposed to those who desire this world and its possessions,

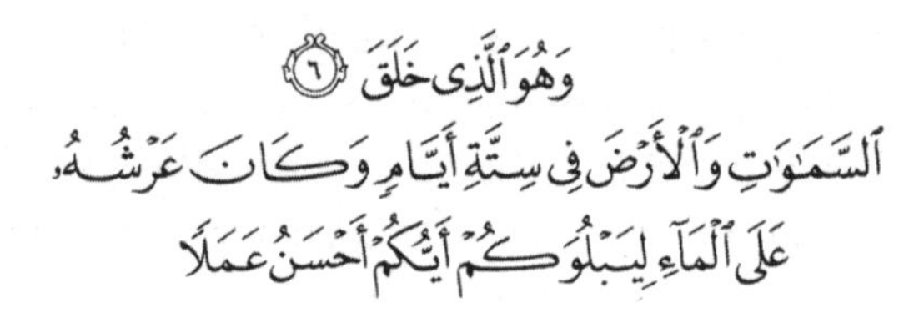

«It is He Who created the heavens and the earth in six days when His Throne was on water, in order to test which of you has the best deeds»

[*Hūd* (11): 7]

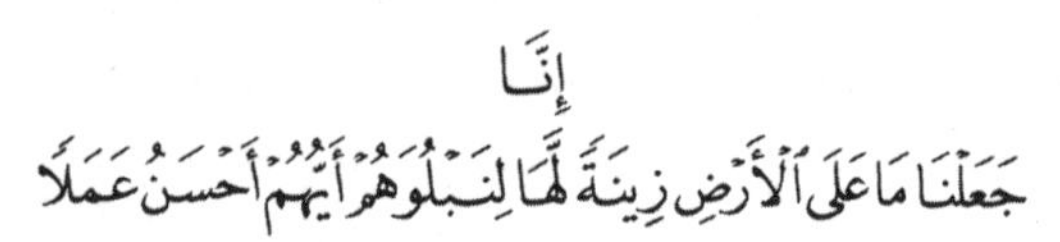

«We made everything on the earth adornment for it so that We could test them to see whose deeds are best»

[*al-Kahf* (18): 7]

ٱلَّذِى خَلَقَ ٱلْمَوْتَ وَٱلْحَيَوٰةَ لِيَبْلُوَكُمْ أَيُّكُمْ أَحْسَنُ عَمَلًا ۚ وَهُوَ ٱلْعَزِيزُ ٱلْغَفُورُ ﴿٢﴾

«He who created death and life to test which of you is best in deed...»

[*al-Mulk* (67): 2]

وَنَبْلُوكُم بِٱلشَّرِّ وَٱلْخَيْرِ فِتْنَةً ۖ وَإِلَيْنَا تُرْجَعُونَ ﴿٣٥﴾

«We test you with both good and evil as a trial; and you will be returned to Us»

[*al-Anbiy,'* (21): 35]

وَلَنَبْلُوَنَّكُمْ حَتَّىٰ نَعْلَمَ
ٱلْمُجَٰهِدِينَ مِنكُمْ وَٱلصَّٰبِرِينَ وَنَبْلُوَا۟ أَخْبَارَكُمْ ﴿٣١﴾

«We will test you until We know the true fighters among you and those who are steadfast and test what is reported of you»

[*Muḥammad* (47): 31]

الٓمٓ ﴿١﴾ أَحَسِبَ ٱلنَّاسُ أَن يُتْرَكُوٓا۟ أَن يَقُولُوٓا۟ ءَامَنَّا وَهُمْ لَا
يُفْتَنُونَ ﴿٢﴾ وَلَقَدْ فَتَنَّا ٱلَّذِينَ مِن قَبْلِهِمْ ۖ فَلَيَعْلَمَنَّ ٱللَّهُ ٱلَّذِينَ
صَدَقُوا۟ وَلَيَعْلَمَنَّ ٱلْكَٰذِبِينَ ﴿٣﴾

«Alif Lām Mīm. Do people think that they will be left to say, 'we believe' and will not be tested? We tested those before them so that Allāh would know the truthful and would know the liars»

[*al-'Ankabūt* (29): 1-3]

When Messenger are sent to them, people fall into one of two categories - believer and disbeliever, and both are tried. As for the believer, he will necessarily undergo trial and tribulation so that it becomes clear as to whether he is truthful in his claim or not. If he is not truthful, he will turn on his heels and flee from tribulation. If he is truthful, he will remain firm and the tribulation will serve to increase him in faith. Allāh, Exalted is He, says,

وَلَمَّا رَءَا ٱلْمُؤْمِنُونَ ٱلْأَحْزَابَ قَالُوا۟ هَٰذَا مَا وَعَدَنَا ٱللَّهُ وَرَسُولُهُۥ
وَصَدَقَ ٱللَّهُ وَرَسُولُهُۥ ۚ وَمَا زَادَهُمْ إِلَّآ إِيمَٰنًا وَتَسْلِيمًا ﴿٢٢﴾

«When the believers saw the Confederates they

said, 'this is what Allāh and His Messenger promised us. Allāh and His Messenger told us the truth.' It only increased them in faith and submission»

[*al-Aḥzāb* (33): 22]

As for the disbeliever, he will be tried in the Hereafter with the punishment. Everyone will face tribulation in this life, in the *Barzakh* and on the Day of Judgment; however the tribulation faced by the believer is relatively less than that of the disbeliever. Allāh allows the believer to bear the tribulation by virtue of his faith and nourishes him with *ṣabr*, firmness (*thabāt*), *riḍā* and acceptance such as would lighten the burden of tribulation. As for the disbeliever, the hypocrite and sinner, tribulation weighs down heavily on them and stretches on. Therefore the tribulation faced by the believer is light and short whereas the tribulation faced by the disbeliever is burdensome and prolonged.

10. Man is a social creature, he must live amongst other people. People all possess intent, imagination and beliefs, as such they will require him to conform to these. If he does not agree with them they will harm or punish him, if he does agree with them he will be harmed or punished via another means. Man must co-exist with other men and he will always be in a state of conforming with them or opposing them. In agreeing with them lies punishment if what is agreed upon is false and in opposing them lies punishment; however there is no doubt that the pain that results from opposing them in their falsehood is lighter and easier to bear than the pain that will result from conforming with them.

So whoever is asked to conform to another in oppression, sin, false witness or the likes, let him reflect on this principle. He knows that if he does not conform, he will be harmed, but he also knows that the final end and victory is for him if he shows *ṣabr* and *taqwā*; if he does conform, he may well be saved from punishment but soon to follow it will be a punishment greater than that which he sought to avoid!

Understanding this principle is one of the most beneficial things; a small amount of punishment would be followed by never ending delight and felicity and a small amount of relief and pleasure could be followed by eternal punishment. Allāh is the One who grants accord.

11. The tribulation that the servant is afflicted with affects one of four things: himself - either by death or something less than that; his property; his honour; or his family and those beloved to him. The severest of these is tribulation in oneself.

It is well known that everybody will die and the goal of the believer is that he be martyred in the cause of Allāh for that is the most noble of deaths and the easiest. The martyr will feel the pain of death as if it were but the bite of a flea. Hence, whoever thinks martyrdom to be a tribulation greater than that of death on ones bed is ignorant. No indeed, martyrdom is the easiest form of death, the most noble and exalted; the one who flees from it thinks that through flight his lifespan will increase but Allāh has proved this notion false,

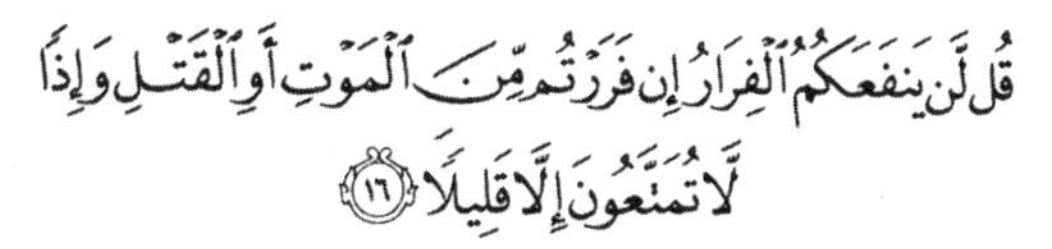

«Say: 'flight will not benefit you if you try to run away from death or being killed. Then you will enjoin only a short respite'»

[*al-Aḥzāb* (33): 16]

Here Allāh, Exalted is He, informs us that running away from martyrdom is of no benefit, and even if were of benefit, that benefit would only be slight for the one fleeing must die, hence this person has missed out on a great deal of good in order to acquire something very slight. Then Allāh says,

قُلْ مَن ذَا الَّذِي يَعْصِمُكُم مِّنَ اللَّهِ إِنْ أَرَادَ بِكُمْ سُوءًا أَوْ أَرَادَ بِكُمْ رَحْمَةً وَلَا يَجِدُونَ لَهُم مِّن دُونِ اللَّهِ وَلِيًّا وَلَا نَصِيرًا ﴿١٧﴾

«Say: 'who is going to shield you from Allāh if He desires evil for you or desires mercy for you?' They will find no one to protect or help them besides Allāh...»

[*al-Aḥzāb* (33): 17]

This person ran away from death thinking it to be bad for him, but Allāh informs him that there is no one who could shield him from Allāh, were He to have desired evil for him; indeed he could be fleeing from martyrdom and fall into something much greater.

The same applies to tribulation of wealth, honour and in body. Whoever is miserly and does not spend in the cause of Allāh, Allāh will take that wealth away from him or restrict it such that he spends it in ways that neither benefit his life in this world nor the Hereafter. If the person hoards the wealth, Allāh would prevent him from taking pleasure from it, and after his death it will merely be passed on to someone else; hence he will bear its sin and the inheritor will feel the joy of acquiring it. The same applies to one who prefers not to employ his body and honour in the way of Allāh in order to save it from weariness and fatigue; Allāh would instead cause him to employ his body, weary it and fatigue it many times over, in other than His cause and good pleasure. This is something that man knows through practical experience.

Abū Hāzim said, 'the one who does not fear Allāh, in trying to benefit from his dealing with people, will never attain anything greater than that attained by the one who does fear Allāh in his trying to perfect taqwā.'

Consider the case of Iblīs, he refused to prostrate to Ādam thinking that by doing so he was submitting to him and humiliating himself. He sought to ennoble himself but Allāh caused him to become the most despicable of creation, a servant to the sinners and transgressors amongst the progeny of Ādam. Consider also the case of the idol-worshippers, they haughtily refused to follow a human Messenger and worship one God, Glorious is He, and instead chose to worship gods made of stone!

The same applies to everyone who refuses to humble himself before Allāh, or use what he has in order to please Him, or exert his energies in obedience to Him; inevitably he will humble himself before something that is incomparable to Allāh and spend his wealth and energies in trying to please it - by way of punishment. Some of the Salaf would say, 'whoever refuses to lift a step in coming to the aid of his brother, Allāh will cause him to lift many steps in disobeying Him.'

Now in order to complete this discussion, we will mention the actual goal that is desired of one; all that has preceded is merely a means to attaining this goal. The goal is the love of Allāh, Glorious is He, taking comfort and solace with Him, ardently desiring to meet Him and to be pleased with Him. This is the essence of the religion and essence of ones deeds and desires. Cognisance of Allāh, knowledge of His Names, Attributes and Actions are from the greatest of objectives; worshipping Him is the most noble deed: praising Him through His Names and Attributes and glorfying Him is the most noble speech; and all of this constitutes the foundation of the upright and sound religion, the religion of Ibrāhīm (*alayhis-Salām*). Allāh, Exalted is He, says to His Messenger,

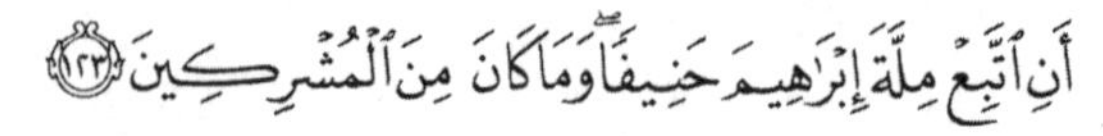

«Follow the religion of Ibrāhīm, a man of pure natural belief. He was not of the polytheists.»
[*an-Naḥl* (16): 123]

The Prophet (ﷺ) would advise his Companions to say upon awakening,

> We have awoken upon the pure natural way of Islām; upon the statement of sincerity; the religion of our Prophet, Muḥammad, the religion of our father, Ibrāhīm, the devout Muslim who was not of the polytheists.

This is the reality behind the testification that none has the right to be worshipped save Allāh, it is upon this that the religion of Islām is constructed, this is the religion of all the Prophets and Messengers and there is no other religion which Allāh will accept,

وَمَن يَبْتَغِ غَيْرَ الْإِسْلَامِ
دِينًا فَلَن يُقْبَلَ مِنْهُ وَهُوَ فِي الْآخِرَةِ مِنَ الْخَاسِرِينَ ﴿٨٥﴾

«If anyone desires a religion other than Islām, it will not be accepted of him and in the Hereafter he will be among the losers»
[*Āli 'Imrān* (3): 85]

Glossary of Arabic Terms

Āyah: pl. *āyāt*. Sign, miracle, example, lesson, verse.

ʿAbd: pl. *ʿebād*. slave, servant, worshipper.

Abrār: righteous.

Adhān: *fiqh*: the call to prayer.

Barzakh: barrier, obstruction, an isthmus. *fiqh*: a barrier placed between a person who has deceased and this worldly life.

Bidʿah: innovation, *fiqh*: that which is newly introduced into the religion of Allāh.

Dīn: religion, way of life.

Dhikr: remembrance, *fiqh*: making mention of Allāh.

Duʿā: supplication, invocation.

Fasād: corruption, decay, and invalidity.

Fatwā: *fiqh*: legal ruling.

Fisq: pl. *fusūq*. Immorality, transgression, wickedness.

Fitnah: pl. *fitan*. Trial, tribulation, civil strife.

Ḥāfidh: pl. *ḥuffādh*. Ḥadīth Master, commonly referred to one who has memorised at least 100 000 *aḥādīth*.

Ḥadīth: pl. *aḥādīth*, speech, report, account. *fiqh*: a narration describing the sayings, actions, character, physical description and tacit approval of the Prophet (ﷺ).

Īmān: faith that also comprises a meaning of submission. Its place is the heart, the tongue and the limbs and it increases with obedience and decreases with disobedience.

Jinn: another creation besides mankind who are invisible to us. They are also subject to the laws of Islām and will be judged in the Hereafter according to how they lived in this life.

Kāfir: a rejecter of faith, disbeliever.

Khalīfah: pl. *khulafā*. Successor, representative. *fiqh*: of the Prophet (ﷺ), head of the Islāmic state. Also called *Amīr al-Muʿminīn* or Leader of the Believers.

Khuṭbah: sermon, lecture. *fiqh*: Friday sermon.

Munāfiq: hypocrite. *fiqh*: one who outwardly displays Islām but inwardly conceals disbelief. This is the worst type of hypocrisy and its possessor is the worst type of disbeliever, there are other lesser types.

Qiblah: *fiqh*: direction to which the Muslims pray, towards the *ka'bah*.

RaḍiyAllāhu 'anhu/'anhā/'anhum/'anhumā: may Allāh be pleased with him/her/them/both of them.

Ṣabr: patience, steadfastness.

Ṣaḥīḥ: healthy, sound, authentic, correct. A ḥadīth that has met the criteria of authenticity and can be used as a legal proof.

Ṣalāh: *fiqh*: the second pillar of Islām, the prayer.

Salaf: predecessors, commonly employed to refer to the first three generations of Muslims.

Shahādah: testification, witness. The declaration that none has the right to be worshipped save Allāh and that Muḥammad (ﷺ) is the Messenger of Allāh.

Shayṭān: Satan, Iblīs, a devil.

Shirk: polytheism, associating partners with Allāh in matters that are exclusive to Allāh.

Sunnah: habit, customary practice, norm and usage as sanctioned by tradition. *fiqh*: the sayings, commands, prohibitions, actions, and tacit approvals of the Prophet (ﷺ).

Sūrah: chapter of the Qur'ān.

Ṭāghut: all that is falsely worshipped besides Allāh.

Taqwā: fearful awareness of Allāh, pious dedication, being careful not to transgress the bounds set by Allāh.

Tawakkul: trust and absolute reliance.

Tawḥīd: the foundation stone of Islām, the absolute belief in the Oneness of Allāh - His being the sole Creator and Sustainer, His being the only One deserving worship and His being unique with respect to His Names and Attributes.

Ummah: nation, the Muslim nation.

Zakāh: *fiqh*: one of the pillars of Islām, an obligatory tax levied on a Muslim wealth subject to certain criteria.

Ẓālim: one who commits *ẓulm*: injustice, harm, transgression either against Allāh, himself or another creation.